HOCKEY NOW!

ELEVENTH EDITION

THE BIGGEST STARS OF THE NHL

MIKE RYAN

FIREFLY BOOKS

For Pip.

A FIREFLY BOOK

Published by Firefly Books Ltd. 2022

First printing

Library of Congress Control Number: 2022942628

Library and Archives Canada Cataloguing in Publication
Title: Hockey now! : the biggest stars of the NHL / Mike Ryan.
Names: Ryan, Mike, 1974- author.
Description: Eleventh edition. | Includes index.
Identifiers: Canadiana 2022039167X | ISBN 9780228103875 (softcover)
Subjects: LCSH: National Hockey League—Biography. | LCSH: Hockey players—
    Biography. | LCSH: Hockey players—Pictorial works. | LCGFT: Biographies.
Classification: LCC GV848.5.A1 L455 2022 | DDC 796.962092/2—dc23

Published in the United States by
Firefly Books (U.S.) Inc.
P.O. Box 1338, Ellicott Station
Buffalo, New York 14205

Published in Canada by
Firefly Books Ltd.
50 Staples Avenue, Unit 1
Richmond Hill, Ontario L4B 0A7

Cover and interior design: Kimberley Young, Hartley Millson and Stacey Cho
Front cover: Danny Murphy/Icon Sportswire: Pietrangelo
        Roy K. Miller/Icon Sportswire: Vasilevskiy
        Gregory Fisher/Icon Sportswire: Crosby
        Rich Graessle/Icon Sportswire: McDavid
        Curtis Comeau/Icon Sportswire: Matthews
        Joshua Sarner/Icon Sportswire: Panarin, Makar
Back cover: Gerry Angus/Icon Sportswire: Josi
        Jeanine Leech/Icon Sportswire: Shesterkin
        Randy Litzinger/Icon Sportswire: McAvoy

Printed in Canada

Canada We acknowledge the financial support of the Government of Canada.

TABLE OF CONTENTS

INTRODUCTION

The last edition of *Hockey Now!* came out in 2019. Not much has happened since then. Just a global pandemic, a long suspension of the NHL season followed by a qualifying round and playoffs waged in two hermetically sealed bubbles in Edmonton and Toronto in August and September 2020. We also had another delayed season with a drastic realignment keeping everyone on their respective sides of the border, as some played to full houses and others to covered seats and a smattering of arena staff in funeral silence.

At the start of the 2021–22 season, it was still newsworthy for a player to test positive for COVID-19, as the season wore on, it was unusual if they didn't. Let's just assume all the players in this book had it at some point, it'll save time and ink.

The season also kicked off with the bravery of Kyle Beach, who spoke about his history of abuse. Many people in the Chicago Blackhawks organization and beyond lost their jobs as a result, and rightfully so.

Another stain on the game that hasn't fully washed out is racism. Nazem Kadri faced some online Islamophobia after an incident in the 2022 playoffs but answered emphatically with a hat trick the following game, and then by becoming the first Muslim to lift the Stanley Cup. Jordan Subban was also on the receiving end of a racial taunt in a January ECHL game, with older brother P.K. and the vast majority of the people in hockey rallying to support him.

The NHL supported Black Lives Matter and Black History Month. Pioneer Willie O'Ree had his number retired by the Boston Bruins in January 2022 on the 64th anniversary of the day he broke the NHL's color barrier, and Herb Carnegie, long considered the best Black player never to play in the NHL, will join him posthumously in the Hall of Fame. Mike Grier also made history as the first Black general manager in the NHL when the San Jose Sharks named him to the post in July 2022.

Women are finally making their way to positions of power too. Two of the best female players in history are now employed by traditional rivals — Marie-Philip Poulin in the Montreal Canadiens' player development department and Hayley Wickenheiser as the Toronto Maple Leafs' new assistant general manager, the same position Émilie Castonguay holds with the Vancouver Canucks.

As for the lucky few who made this book, it was a balance of past accomplishments, the season unfolding as I wrote it, and future projections, broken down by position and division.

And many worthy players didn't quite make the cut. On either end of the career spectrum, Patrice Bergeron won his fifth Selke Trophy but didn't get in because there was too much retirement speculation, while Calder Trophy winner Moritz Seider doesn't have the body of work just yet. Both play in the Atlantic Division, where there's a fine young crop of players, especially among forwards, who will surely shake up the list next time around.

Speaking of young talent, will Quinn Hughes or Matthew Tkachuk be joined by a brother (or two) next time? Three years ago, Adam Fox and Cale Makar, the last two Norris Trophy winners, were virtual unknowns. With a Stanley Cup and Conn Smythe Trophy to boot, Makar is now considered the gold standard for defensemen and a shining example of the skill level in the NHL.

Makar is our cover star, joined by Artemi Panarin, who had narrowly missed the cut in both of the two editions I've written. He was an easy choice this time and in the news in recent seasons for all the wrong reasons. After writing in support of Alexei Navalny, an opponent and critic of Vladimir Putin, he was forced to return to Russia to answer false accusations and protect his family. Backing Putin also took some of the luster off of Alex Ovechkin as he chases Wayne Gretzky for the all-time goal-scoring record.

World events conspired to take the focus away from hockey and reminded me to keep sports in proper perspective, but the 2022 postseason sure was a happy distraction.

After the highest scoring weekend in hockey history at the end of the regular season, it was the most

offense the first round has seen since the 1980s and 1990s. The games were wild, but there was also a comfortable predictability with the Maple Leafs and Hart Trophy-winner Auston Matthews making their traditional first round exit.

After waiting 31 years, the Battle of Alberta gave us a 9-6 opening game of round two, as well as a series with a 132-foot goal and the fastest four goals in playoff history. That was almost matched by the 8-6 game the Edmonton Oilers also lost in the opener of the Western Conference Final. Connor McDavid and Leon Draisaitl were swept in the Stanley Cup semifinal but still finished first and second in playoff scoring!

In the end, a loaded Colorado Avalanche halted the mini-dynasty of the equally stacked Tampa Bay Lightning, who had crushed the dreams of Canadiens and (some) Canadians a year prior.

The Canadiens had an improbable and inspiring run to the 2021 Stanley Cup Final after becoming champions of the one-off North Division, a feather in their very decorated chapeau. It breathed spring life into a city that had endured some of the strictest lockdown measures on the planet, but it essentially ended captain Shea Weber's career, and Carey Price missed almost the entire year following with a knee injury and time spent in the NHL's player assistance program. His choice to open up about his mental health earned him the Bill Masterton Trophy.

The Canadiens plummeted to the bottom of the standings, and they took Juraj Slafkovsky with the first overall draft choice in 2022, their fifth in franchise history and first since 1980. One of those picks was icon Guy Lafleur, who the hockey world lost in 2022, just days after another one of best goal-scorers the game has ever seen, Mike Bossy.

Price still has a Stanley Cup-sized hole in his very deep resume, and the city and country await their first championship since 1993. No pressure, kid.

That's just one of the myriad storylines to watch until the 12th edition of *Hockey Now!* comes out. If it's released on time and the focus is simply on hockey, I'll consider myself lucky, as I have in writing this one. I hope you enjoy it.

ATLANTIC DIVISION

FIRST TEAM

8	**JONATHAN HUBERDEAU**	Panthers	Left Wing
10	**NIKITA KUCHEROV**	Lightning	Right Wing
12	**AUSTON MATTHEWS**	Maple Leafs	Center
14	**VICTOR HEDMAN**	Lightning	Defense
16	**CHARLIE McAVOY**	Bruins	Defense
18	**ANDREI VASILEVSKIY**	Lightning	Goalie

SECOND TEAM

20	**STEVEN STAMKOS**	Lightning	Center
22	**BRAD MARCHAND**	Bruins	Left Wing
24	**MITCHELL MARNER**	Maple Leafs	Right Wing
26	**AARON EKBLAD**	Panthers	Defense
28	**MORGAN RIELLY**	Maple Leafs	Defense
30	**CAREY PRICE**	Canadiens	Goalie

TAXI SQUAD

JONATHAN HUBERDEAU

Panthers | Left Wing | 11

Like a lot of kids from Saint-Jerome, Quebec, Jonathan Huberdeau was a massive Montreal Canadiens fan. The Bell Centre was less than an hour southeast, but the family would take an annual RV trip to go watch the Habs play the Florida Panthers in Sunrise. Little did they know it would become a regular journey.

Chosen 18th overall in the 2009 Quebec Major Junior Hockey League draft by the Saint John Sea Dogs, Huberdeau planned to play hockey in the U.S., but America's loss was New Brunswick's gain. He had 43 goals and set team records for assists (62) and points (105) to go with a league-leading plus-59 in 2010–11, and Saint John won its first league title. He took home the Guy Lafleur Trophy as QMJHL playoff MVP, then added the Stafford Smythe Trophy for Memorial Cup MVP after the Sea Dogs became the first team from

Atlantic Canada to win the tournament.

Taken third overall by the Florida Panthers in the 2011 NHL draft, Huberdeau was leading the team in preseason scoring that fall, but after being flattened in the final exhibition game, the team decided he wasn't ready for the physicality of the NHL.

Back in Saint John, Huberdeau lit up the Q with 72 points (30 goals, 47 assists) in 37 regular-season games, followed by 21 points in 15 QMJHL playoff games as the Sea Dogs repeated in 2012.

A lockout delayed the start of the 2012–13 NHL season, so Huberdeau was in Saint John once again. He had 45 points in 30 games when he finally had a chance to join the Panthers in January 2013. He scored on his first NHL shot before adding two assists in his debut game, and ended the season with 31 points in

48 games and the first Calder Trophy in team history.

Hip surgery in the offseason took a bite out of Huberdeau, and he had just nine goals as a sophomore in 2013–14. In 2014 the Panthers hired Gerard Gallant, Huberdeau's junior coach, and the partnership paid off over the next two seasons.

"He was 155 pounds when I had him, but he was a great hockey player with a lot of competitiveness," Gallant said at the time. "He's not just going to be a good hockey player but a great one in this league."

Gallant knew what he was talking about. Huberdeau led the Panthers in assists (39) and points (54) in the 2014–15 season, then had 59 points (20 goals, 39 assists) in 2015–16 to help Florida finish first in the Atlantic Division.

In 2016–17 Huberdeau had his Achilles tendon sliced and missed 51 games. He returned with 69 points in 2017–18, then set new career highs with 30 goals, 62 assists and 92 points in 2018–19. He tied for 12th in NHL scoring, but it wasn't very satisfying.

"You can't be excited about 92 points when we didn't make the playoffs," said Huberdeau. "Yes, it's fun personally, but I'd rather have 70 and make the playoffs."

Now a solid 202 pounds, Huberdeau has missed only three games since returning from the career-threatening injury and continues to be among the elite scorers in the NHL, while bringing the Panthers up with him.

Florida only qualified for the postseason once in his first eight years, but after getting 61 points in 55 games of the shortened 2020–21 season, Huberdeau had eight assists and 10 points in a six-game loss to the state rival Tampa Bay Lightning in the first round.

In 2021–22, Huberdeau and the Panthers took it up a notch. On April 3, he earned his 97th point in his 69th game to pass Aleksander Barkov for the highest-scoring season in franchise history. He finished first in the NHL with 85 assists, shattering the NHL record of 70 for left wingers that had stood since 1992–93, tied Johnny Gaudreau for second in the NHL with 115 points, and finished fifth in Hart Trophy voting.

In the playoffs, the President's Trophy-winning Panthers got their first series win since 1996, but Tampa Bay swept them in the second round.

Huberdeau finished the season in Panthers' history in games played (671), assists (415) and points (613). That kind of offense usually brings fame and money, but the low-key Huberdeau toiled in relative anonymity on a bargain $5.9 million a year contract that ends in 2022–23. But he's on the hockey world's radar now after a mega-trade sent him to the Calgary Flames for Matthew Tkachuk.

Replacing Tkachuk and fellow 115-point scorer Johnny Gaudreau, who left in free agency, will be a tall order, and a Florida reporter said Huberdeau wasn't "particularly happy with how everything played out."

But a motivated Huberdeau in the last year of his contract should be fun to watch, and a hockey-mad fan base can convince the Canadian to stay home.

Memorial Cup champion and MVP with the Saint John Sea Dogs in 2011

Won the 2013 Calder Trophy

Played in two NHL All-Star Games (2020, 2022)

Led the NHL in assists (85) and finished tied for second in points (115) in 2021–22

Florida Panthers franchise leader in games played (671), assists (415) and points (613)

NIKITA KUCHEROV

Lightning | Right Wing | 86

At 13, Lionel Messi was signed by FC Barcelona and brought over from Argentina because the team agreed to pay for his medical treatment when his home side wouldn't — one of the wisest investments in sports history. There are parallels to Nikita Kucherov, who's making his own case as the best on Earth in his chosen sport.

An undersized winger with CSKA Moscow's youth team, the native of Maykop, Russia, was lightly regarded by NHL scouts. Even after a tournament record 21 points in seven games at the 2011 Under-18 World Championship, he still lasted until 58th in the draft that year, when he was chosen by the Tampa Bay Lightning.

That's when the problems with CSKA began. Kucherov had injuries to both shoulders, but the team didn't believe him and refused to pay for surgery. His agent approached then-Lightning general manager Steve Yzerman days after the draft, and Yzerman agreed to look after Kucherov's treatment and recovery.

Kucherov decided to void the rest of his contract with CSKA and came over to North America as a 19-year-old in 2012. He made his NHL debut in November 2013 and scored his first NHL goal on his first shot of his first shift in his first game, but spent parts of the season and playoffs learning from the press box.

Playing a full slate of games in 2014–15, Kucherov tied for the NHL lead with a plus-38 rating and added 22 points in 26 playoff games to help the Lightning reach the Stanley Cup Final.

The following season, Kucherov had 11 goals in 17 playoff games as the Lightning reached Game 7 of the Eastern Conference Final, and he became just the third player in NHL history to score 10 or more goals in multiple playoffs before turning 23, joining Jeremy Roenick and Evgeni Malkin.

In 2017–18 Kucherov had an even 100 points, good for third in the NHL, and he had 17 points in 17 playoff games as the Lightning lost in Game 7 of the Eastern Conference Final again.

In 2018 Kucherov agreed to an eight-year, $76 million contract extension, which immediately seemed like a bargain. His 128 points in 2018–19 were 12 ahead of Connor McDavid in second, the highest total since Mario Lemieux in 1995–96, and the most ever by a Russian, breaking the record set by Alexander Mogilny in 1992–93. His 87 assists tied Jaromir Jagr's NHL record for most by a winger in one season, and two days after turning 26, Kucherov won the Hart Trophy, the Art Ross Trophy and the Ted Lindsay Award.

"The whole thing is about the Stanley Cup. That's why you play the game. You want to win. It doesn't matter about the individual stuff," said Kucherov after his trophy haul, and he took care of that a year later.

Kucherov led the 2020 playoffs in the bubble with 27 assists and 34 points in 25 games, and the Lightning won their first championship since 2004, beating the Dallas Stars in the Final.

Following offseason hip surgery, Kucherov missed the entire realigned and shortened 2020–21 season, offering the Lightning cap relief on the long-term injured reserve. Back just in time for the playoffs and skating into an ethically gray but perfectly legal salary situation, he dominated.

Kucherov scored two goals in the first game and finished with 24 assists and 32 points in 23 games. Tampa Bay won its second straight Stanley Cup, and he became the sixth player to lead the postseason in scoring in consecutive seasons. At the press conference after the victory over the Canadiens, a shirtless Kucherov drained a beer while taking shots at Montreal fans, suggesting they celebrated their one win in the Final a little too hard.

Kucherov took a chunk of the 2021–22 season off too after suffering a lower body injury, but still had 44 assists and 69 points in 47 games. Going for the first three-peat since the New York Islanders in the 1980s, the Lightning were dethroned by the Colorado Avalanche in the Stanley Cup Final. Kucherov was fourth with 27 playoff points in 23 games, despite playing with a knee injury.

In the 2022 postseason, Kucherov also became just the sixth player with 20 career playoff games with at least three points. Since 2015, he has 153 points in 134 playoff games, 55 points ahead of teammate Victor Hedman for first among all players.

"It's amazing," said Lightning captain Steven Stamkos. "I've played with some Hall of Fame players, but this guy is special. And you have to appreciate while you're watching it because it's pretty remarkable what he's able to do, especially this time of year."

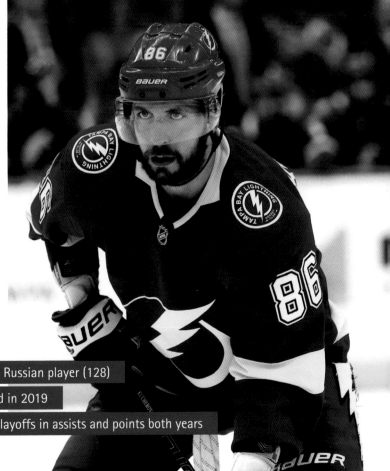

Played in three NHL All-Star Games (2017, 2018, 2019)

Holds the single-season record for the most points ever by a Russian player (128)

Won the Hart Trophy, Art Ross Trophy and Ted Lindsay Award in 2019

Two-time Stanley Cup champion (2020, 2021), leading the playoffs in assists and points both years

AUSTON MATTHEWS

Maple Leafs | Center | 34

under the unorthodox tutelage of Boris Dorozhenko, who fled the Soviet Union to run the Mexican national hockey team.

When Matthews was 17, he continued on the road less traveled, eschewing college or major junior hockey for a year in Europe. Two days shy of being eligible for the 2015 NHL Entry Draft, he chose to play in Zurich for the ZSC Lions in the National League A, Switzerland's top professional circuit, where he had 24 goals and 46 points in 36 games, the highest totals in league history for a player under 20. Meanwhile, in Toronto, the Maple Leafs had finished last in the NHL in 2015–16. The odds and draft lottery balls smiled upon them and they chose Matthews number one overall, their first top pick since they drafted Wendel Clark in 1985.

If there was any doubt Matthews could make it at the highest level he erased it in his first NHL game. On October 12, 2016, against the Ottawa Senators, Matthews had the greatest NHL debut in nearly 100 years, becoming the first player in modern NHL history (since 1943–44) to score four goals in his first game. On March 7, 2017, he broke Clark's 31-year-old franchise rookie record with his 35th goal of the season, and on April 8 he scored his 40th to clinch the Leafs' first playoff berth since 2013.

Matthews was the fourth player in NHL history to score 40 goals in a season before his 20th birthday, and he joined Mats Sundin as the only Leaf in the past 22 years with at least 40. He capped it off by winning the Calder Trophy, the Leafs first since Brit Selby in 1966.

All Matthews has done since is put the puck in the back of the net. He's had four seasons of 40-plus goals, already tied with Darryl Sittler for the most in franchise history, and he would likely have six if not for injuries. In the pandemic-shortened 2020–21 season, he won the Maurice Richard Trophy with 41 goals in 52 games, the first Leaf to lead the NHL in goals in 74 years. Toronto was first in the North Division.

No NHL team is more thirsty for success than the Toronto Maple Leafs. For the past 55 years, they've been wandering the desert in search of a Stanley Cup. But a savior arrived from Arizona of all places, which is about as far away from Toronto as possible, in hockey terms.

Auston Matthews is a child of the NHL's southern expansion. He was raised by his Mexican mother, Ema, and Californian father, Brian, in Scottsdale, Arizona, where he was seduced by the speed of Coyotes games.

Matthews learned the game on Ozzie Ice, a facility with two small rinks created by pipeline entrepreneur Dwayne Osadchuk. He played countless hours of 3-on-3 with older kids, while sharpening his skating

Facing the Montreal Canadiens in the first round of the 2021 playoffs, the Maple Leafs were preordained as Kings of the North and took a three games to one lead to prove it. But Montreal fought back and won two games in overtime before eliminating Toronto in Game 7. Matthews had one goal in the series and didn't score after Game 2.

The 2021–22 season went a long way to making people forget about that collapse. After a slow start while recovering from offseason wrist surgery, Matthews had a mind-boggling 57 goals in 61 games, including a streak of 51 goals in 50 games.

Matthews shattered Rick Vaive's franchise record of 54 goals in a season and became the first NHL player in a decade with 60, and he only needed 73 games to do it. He finished the season with 106 points, tied for sixth in the NHL and the fourth highest single-season total in team history.

A similar script followed in the 2022 postseason, however. Matthews had two goals in Game 1 of the first round but only two more the rest of the way as Toronto lost to the Tampa Bay Lightning in seven games. They've been eliminated in the first postseason series every year Matthews has played.

Matthews is on deck to take over from Alex Ovechkin as best active goal-scorer in the world — with 259 he's four goals ahead of the Russian for first in the NHL since he joined the league — he's also assuming his title of playoff underachiever. It followed Ovechkin around until he finally made it out of the second round and won the Stanley Cup in his 13th season. Leafs Nation might not have that kind of patience, they're already gnashing their teeth at the thought of Matthews leaving when his five-year, $58.17 million contract expires in 2024.

Like Ovechkin in his early years, Matthews has started to pile up individual awards. With a deep tan, long hair and wide-open collar, he accepted his second Maurice Richard Trophy, the Ted Lindsay Award and the Hart Trophy in 2022. It was just the third time a Maple Leaf has been named MVP and first since Ted Kennedy in 1955, 67 years ago.

But it's 1967 that Toronto fans are more concerned about. Arguably the most talented player to ever wear the Maple Leaf, if Matthews helps break that losing streak there will be no more questions.

VICTOR HEDMAN

Lightning | Defense | 77

When 18-year-old Victor Hedman joined the Tampa Bay Lightning after being drafted second overall in 2009, it was only the second organization he'd ever played in. From the age of six, he'd played in the legendary MoDo system in his hometown of Ornskoldsvik, Sweden. "Just a good hockey town, rinks everywhere, outdoor and indoor," said Hedman. "You're skating for hours and hours, you go home to eat and then you go out again. Get the lights on when it gets dark. Just all about hockey."

The main employer is the Holmen paper mill, which sponsors MoDo and is where Hedman's dad, Olle, worked when he wasn't managing equipment for the hockey team. A town of just 27,000 people that sits six hours north of Stockholm, Ornskoldsvik has produced NHL stars Markus Naslund, Henrik and

Daniel Sedin, and Hedman's favorite, Peter Forsberg, among many others.

Between organized and impromptu hockey, Hedman learned to skate through his awkward phases as he grew into his 6-foot-6 frame. Gawky growing up, the defenseman is now 241 pounds and one of the smoothest skaters in the NHL.

After winning silver medals with Sweden at the World Juniors in 2008 and 2009 and Rookie of the Year in the Swedish Hockey League in 2009 as a teenager, Hedman made the move to Florida. "It's probably the toughest . . . to come into this league as an 18-year-old defenseman," said Lightning captain Steven Stamkos. "There were some tough years, but we went through tough years as a team."

By 2015, Hedman was making his case for best

defenseman in the game. Averaging 26 minutes a night in the playoffs and shutting down Jonathan Toews in the Stanley Cup Final, Hedman was a strong Conn Smythe candidate, but Tampa Bay fell to the Chicago Blackhawks in six games.

In 2016–17 Hedman led all defensemen with a career-best 56 assists in 79 games. He also had career highs in goals (16) and points (72), led the NHL with 29 power-play assists and ranked second with 33 power-play points and was a Norris Trophy finalist.

The following season, Hedman scored 17 goals, a career high that put him in a three-way tie for first among defensemen. He added 46 assists, while also setting new career bests with a plus-32 rating and an average of 25:51 minutes of ice time a game. He became the first Lightning player to win the Norris.

The recognition took some of the sting out of losing for the third time in Game 7 of the Eastern Conference Final, each to the eventual champion. The 2019 playoffs might have been even more heartbreaking, and motivating. After tying an NHL record with 62 regular-season wins to stroll to the Presidents' Trophy, the Lightning were swept by the Columbus Blue Jackets in the first round.

Tampa Bay emerged from the 2020 playoff bubble as Stanley Cup champions, defeating the Dallas Stars for the team's first title since 2004. Hedman averaged 26:20 of ice time and scored 10 goals, just the third defenseman in league history to reach the mark and the most since the New York Rangers' Brian Leetch had 11 in 1994.

"I think I told him I loved him a hundred times," said an injured Stamkos after Hedman won the Conn Smythe Trophy for playoff MVP.

In the 2021 postseason, Hedman had 18 points in 23 games, and the Lightning repeated as champions by defeating the Montreal Canadiens, normally Atlantic Division rivals brought together in the Final by pandemic realignment.

Offensively, the 2021–22 season was Hedman's best yet, with 20 goals, 65 assists and 85 points in 82 games. It was his third year in a row of coming third among defensemen in scoring, and his 603 regular season points are third since he entered the league. It was also his sixth straight year (and counting) of being a Norris finalist.

The Lightning's mini-dynasty ended with a loss to the Colorado Avalanche in the 2022 Stanley Cup Final, but after 19 points in 23 games, Hedman's 107 career playoff points lead all defensemen since his first postseason appearance, 38 ahead of second place John Carlson, and he's tied for fourth overall with Evgeni Malkin and Patrice Bergeron.

Already among the pantheon of Ornskoldsvik legends, the bedrock of the Lightning is carving himself into the Mount Rushmore of Swedish hockey.

Awarded the Guldpucken (Golden Puck) as Sweden's best hockey player in 2015

Won gold at the 2017 World Championship

Played in three NHL All-Star Games (2017, 2020, 2022)

Won the Norris Trophy in 2018, and a finalist for six consecutive seasons (2017–2022)

Won the Conn Smythe Trophy in 2020

Two-time Stanley Cup champion (2020, 2021)

CHARLIE McAVOY

Bruins | Defense | 73

Charles A. McAvoy Plumbing & Heating helped install the rink at Long Beach Municipal Ice Arena. It's a family business founded in 1926, and Charlie McAvoy Sr. is a fourth-generation proprietor. He's also father of one of the arena's most famous alumni, Charlie Jr.

The arena is on the southern shore of Long Island near JFK Airport and 20 minutes away from Nassau Coliseum, former home of the New York Islanders. McAvoy Jr. played at the old Islanders practice rink in Syosset with the Long Island Gulls and went to Islanders games with teammate Owen Sillinger when his father, Mike, was on the team. But he grew up a fan of the New York Rangers. It was in the family blood, and his favorite player was Hall of Fame defenseman Brian Leetch. Besides, Long Beach Arena was once a Rangers practice facility, and he also played for the Junior

Rangers, coached by none other than Mark Messier. Ironically, they played on Coliseum ice.

As McAvoy's talents grew, he left the Island and cut across Manhattan to play for the New Jersey Rockets. His eye was on a longer trip, however, to Ann Arbor, Michigan, and the U.S. National Team Development Program (USNTDP).

Heartbroken that he didn't hear from them in his first year of eligibility, McAvoy played his way on and ended up with the USNTDP for two seasons. He made some of his closest companions there, who are now scattered throughout the NHL, and helped Team USA win gold at the 2015 World Under-18 Championship. "It's two years, but it feels like two long years. You go through high school with these guys, so they're your school friends and best friends on the ice. It's really neat. I don't think there's anything like it," says McAvoy.

McAvoy then enrolled at Boston University as a 17-year-old and the freshman led the Terriers defense with 25 points (three goals, 22 assists) in 37 games, enough to convince the Boston Bruins to draft him with the 14th overall pick in 2016.

The following season, McAvoy had 26 points (five goals, 21 assists) in 38 games and was named a First Team All-American. He also earned gold and some more Bruins fans at the 2017 World Junior Championship by beating Canada in Montreal.

After signing a three-year, entry-level contract when the BU season ended, the 19-year-old made his NHL debut in the first round of the 2017 playoffs against the Ottawa Senators.

McAvoy played in all six games of the series, earning three assists and averaging 26:12 of ice time, second among Bruins defensemen behind his partner, the legendary Zdeno Chara.

The following season, McAvoy had 32 points and a plus-20 rating in 63 games, and was named to the NHL All-Rookie Team.

McAvoy played only 54 regular-season games in 2018–19 because of injuries, but he was a force in the postseason. He led the team in average ice time at 24:30 over 23 games, more than two minutes ahead of Torey Krug in second and three more than Chara, as Boston lost to the St. Louis Blues in the seventh game of the Stanley Cup Final.

In 2020–21 McAvoy had 25 assists and 38 points in 51 games and finished fifth in Norris Trophy voting. In the playoffs, the Bruins played the Islanders in the second round, and he faced some heat from friends back home but had seven assists in the six-game loss, and 11 assists and 12 points in 11 postseason games.

After finishing with career-highs in goals (10), assists (46) and points (56) in 2021–22, tied for ninth among NHL defensemen in assists and 11th in points,

McAvoy had five points in six games against the Carolina Hurricanes in the first round of the playoffs. The Bruins lost the series in seven and will be without their number one defenseman to start the 2022–23 season after he underwent shoulder surgery.

Growing up, McAvoy dug trenches for sewer mains, and the 6-foot-1, 211-pound McAvoy isn't afraid to go to them on the ice, although his dad says he didn't get the family's "Irish temper." He's defense-first and can do the dirty work of player once known as a "plumber," but what sets his game apart isn't physicality, it's smooth skating and confidence with the puck. There's no situation on the ice he can't handle.

McAvoy is expected back in December, and with a new eight-year, $76 million contract, it doesn't look like he'll be giving up hockey to become the fifth generation of McAvoy Plumbing anytime soon.

Won gold at the 2015 World Under-18 Championship

Won gold and named to the All-Star Team at the 2017 World Junior Championship

Led all defensemen in points (9) and won bronze at the 2018 World Championship

Named to the NHL All-Rookie Team in 2017–18

ANDREI VASILEVSKIY

Lightning | Goalie | 88

Andrei Vasilevskiy Sr. was a goalie in the old Soviet Superleague's second division who backed up Alexander Tyjnych, himself the backup for legend Vladislav Tretiak on the national team. That connection got Andrei Jr. his first agent. "He was one of those guys who could eat hockey, sleep hockey, breathe hockey," said Tyjnych, who signed Vasilevskiy when he was 15. "My first impression was he had the [guts]. He had the drive to be the best goalie in the world."

Years later, Vasilevskiy has cemented that status.

A native of Tyumen, Russia, Vasilevskiy was the first goalie taken in the 2012 draft when the Tampa Bay Lightning chose him 19th overall. He remained in Russia for the next two years and led his country to bronze medals at the 2013 and 2014 World Juniors, with a goals-against average under 2.00 and a save percentage over .930 in both tournaments. Then at the 2014 World Championship, he allowed only one goal in his two starts as the Russians won gold.

Vasilevskiy made his NHL debut in December 2014 and later that season became the first NHL goalie to earn his first playoff victory in relief in the Stanley Cup Final since the New York Rangers' Lester Patrick in 1928.

"He was just cool, not jittery, not arrogant, [but] self-assured," said analyst and former NHL goalie Kevin Weekes of Vasilevskiy's Stanley Cup debut.

The Lightning sent 6-foot-7, 215-pound starting goalie Ben Bishop to the Los Angeles Kings at the 2017 trade deadline to make way for 6-foot-4, 215-pound Vasilevskiy, and their faith was rewarded in 2017–18. He had a 44-17-3 record, tied for most wins with Connor Hellebuyck, and posted a 2.62 goals-against average and a .920 save percentage. He also tied Vezina Trophy winner Pekka Rinne for the league lead with eight shutouts.

In 2018–19 Vasilevskiy led the NHL with 39 wins, despite missing 14 games with a broken foot, while being fourth with a .925 save percentage and fifth with a 2.40 goals-against average. He was first in the NHL in actual versus expected goals per game and saved nearly one goal per game (0.94) compared to the league average. After finishing third the previous year, Vasilevskiy won the Vezina convincingly over second-place Bishop.

The Lightning's first-round sweep by the Columbus Blue Jackets was especially shocking considering Vasilevskiy had lost back-to-back games only once in the regular season, in a shootout and then in overtime, and finished 13-0-1 after a loss.

That kind of resilience soon came to define Vasilevskiy's postseasons, as the Lightning reigned over the NHL.

Because of the qualifying round of the 2020 playoffs, Vasilevskiy set an NHL record with 18 wins in 25 games

as the Lightning won the Stanley Cup in the playoff bubble. He had a goals-against average of 1.90 and a .927 save percentage, but didn't win the Conn Smythe Trophy. A matching goals-against in the 2021 postseason, an even better .937 save percentage, and a shutout in each of the four series-clinching games earned it for him in 2021 as Tampa Bay repeated.

After beating the Toronto Maple Leafs in the first round of the 2022 playoffs, Vasilevskiy allowed only three goals over a four-game sweep of the Presidents' Trophy-winning Florida Panthers. He then outdueled countryman and 2022 Vezina winner Igor Shesterkin of the New York Rangers in the Eastern Conference Final.

In Tampa Bay's third straight Final, Vasilevskiy allowed 11 goals over the first two games, including seven goals in Game 2 while insisting he stay in the game. It was a rare display of mortality or a tribute to the Avalanche, who dethroned the champions in six games.

Vasilevskiy has now led or tied for first in regular season wins for five years running, and since 2015, his 63 playoff wins are 23 ahead of second place Marc-Andre Fleury and Braden Holtby. But it's his

Won gold at the 2014 World Championship
Named to four NHL All-Star Games (2018, 2019, 2020, 2022)
Named Best Goalkeeper at the World Championship in 2017 and 2019
Won the Vezina Trophy in 2019
Two-time Stanley Cup champion (2020, 2021)
Won the 2021 Conn Smythe Trophy

other postseason numbers that boggle the mind.

Before losing consecutive games to the Rangers, Vasilevskiy had 18 straight wins following a playoff loss, with a .942 save percentage, a 1.49 goals-against average and five shutouts. And over eight series clinching games dating back to the 2020 Cup Final, he allowed a total of two goals.

The regular season numbers are stellar, the postseason stats make "Big Cat" the best in the world right now. The only question is how history will view him.

"Everyone has Roy, Brodeur and Hasek in the top three," says Martin Biron, another former goalie turned analyst. "But by time Vasilevskiy is done, he'll be top five all time."

19

STEVEN STAMKOS

Lightning | Center | 91

with 51 goals in 2009–10. The following season, he helped the Lightning reach the playoffs for the first time in four years, where they lost the Eastern Conference Final in seven games to the Boston Bruins.

Stamkos took home his second goal-scoring crown in 2012 after becoming just the second player since 1996 to score 60 goals and was skating smoothly toward Hall of Fame credentials before injuries began taking their toll.

In 2013–14 Stamkos fractured the tibia in his right leg and missed 45 games. He returned on March 6, 2014, skating out for the first time as the captain of the Lightning, the 10th in franchise history.

After playing the full 82 games in 2014–15 and scoring 43 goals, Stamkos and the Lightning reached the Stanley Cup Final, losing in six games to the Chicago Blackhawks.

Tampa Bay was anticipating another long playoff run in 2015–16 when Stamkos was shut down with blood clots in his shoulder late in the season. He had a rib removed to alleviate the problem and made an inspiring but ultimately futile comeback in Game 7 of the conference final against Pittsburgh.

In a disturbing déjà vu, Stamkos had nine goals and 20 points in 17 games before tearing the lateral meniscus in his right knee in November 2016. He had surgery and missed the remainder of the season.

The franchise cornerstone was back to health and form in 2018–19, playing every game for the first time in four years. His 45 goals were fourth in the NHL, and his 98 points set a new career high. But disappointment inevitably followed.

The Lightning had 62 wins and 128 points, 21 ahead of the second overall Calgary Flames, and they boasted the first trio of 40-plus goal-scorers since 1995–96, so it was stunning when the Columbus Blue Jackets swept them in the first round.

The hockey gods still weren't done doling out disappointment. Stamkos had sports hernia surgery in 2020,

L ife isn't fair. While it can be hard to summon sympathy for millionaire athletes, spare a thought for Steven Stamkos. He's one of hockey's nice guys and true leaders, and he's had more than his fair share of setbacks.

Growing up in Unionville, Ontario, Stamkos started skating at 2 years old and grew up playing hockey with future NHL star John Tavares. The two good friends became the second and third players, after Eric Lindros, to be drafted first overall in both the Ontario Hockey League and NHL.

Stamkos lived up to his 2008 selection by the Tampa Bay Lightning by winning the Maurice Richard Trophy in his second season after leading the league

days before the pandemic shut down the NHL and the world. When the long-delayed playoffs arrived, a compensatory injury kept him out of the lineup, except for 2:47 worth of playing time.

Stamkos scored a goal on his only shot in his one valiant, glorious game in the 2020 playoffs, which lasted five shifts in Game 3 of the Stanley Cup Final against the Dallas Stars. The Lightning won the game and the series, and Stamkos dressed to finally lift the Stanley Cup as captain.

Again, Stamkos missed the final 16 games of the 2020–21 season after knee surgery, but played 23 games in the postseason. He contributed 18 points to the Lightning's second straight championship run, which culminated in a Finals win over the Montreal Canadiens.

The 2021–22 season was a career renaissance for

Stamkos and proof that the 32-year-old still had game after all his injuries. He scored 42 goals and had career highs with 64 assists and 106 points. It was his first time cracking the 100-point barrier and tied him with Hart Trophy-winner Auston Matthews for sixth in the NHL.

Stamkos ended the season with 481 goals and 972 points in 922 games played. He's second in the NHL in goals behind Alex Ovechkin since his NHL debut and fourth in points.

The season didn't end with the first Stanley Cup three-peat since the early 1980s New York Islanders, despite Stamkos best efforts on the ice and behind the scenes. A speech when Tampa Bay were down three games to two and a period away from elimination against Tavares and the Toronto Maple Leafs in the first round inspired a comeback, and his 11 playoff goals tied for the team playoff lead. Two came in the 2-1 win that clinched the Eastern Conference Final over the New York Rangers, but the Lightning fell in the Cup Final to the Colorado Avalanche.

Afterwards, a choked up Stamkos vowed they'd be back. "Who says we're done?" he asked at the press conference after.

It's been asked about him, and answered, so don't count out the team he leads.

Won gold at the 2008 World Junior Championship

Won the Maurice Richard Trophy twice (2010, 2012)

Named to seven NHL All-Star Games (2010, 2012, 2015, 2016, 2018, 2019, 2022)

Won the World Cup of Hockey in 2016

Two-time Stanley Cup champion (2020, 2021)

BRAD MARCHAND

Bruins | Left Wing | 63

Long known as the Little Ball of Hate, he's now one of the NHL's top point producers. And when it comes to Brad Marchand, you can't have the latter without the former.

Having made a name for himself as a trouble-maker before he was a scorer, Marchand's moniker even caught the attention of a U.S. president. When Marchand was at the White House with his Boston Bruins teammates after winning the 2011 Stanley Cup, Barack Obama asked, "What's up with that nickname, man?" For once, Marchand was left speechless.

The nickname was inherited from former NHLer Pat Verbeek, who had 522 career goals and nearly 3,000 penalty minutes, but Marchand has been given plenty of his own. He's been called Squirrel, Weapon of Mass Distraction, Rat, Pigeon, Brat and Nose Face Killah.

His first was Tomahawk, thanks to a two-handed swing that dented an opponent's facemask when he was a 14-year-old in Lower Sackville, Nova Scotia.

Rob O'Brien was in the stands scouting for his Dartmouth Subways major midget team when Marchand took batting practice on his opponent's face. It convinced him to recruit the undersized forward. "I really felt that his temperament could be an asset rather than a detriment. Brad is a real personality on the ice. A lot of coaches tried to beat that out of him, but I encouraged it."

After running roughshod with his midget team, Marchand was a second-round pick of the Moncton Wildcats in the 2004 Quebec Major Junior Hockey League draft. In 2006 Moncton reached the Memorial Cup final, and soon after Boston drafted Marchand in the third round, 71st overall.

Marchand played two more seasons in junior, split between the Val d'Or Foreurs and the Halifax Mooseheads, and won back-to-back gold medals at the World Juniors in 2007 and 2008 before turning pro.

In 2010–11, his first full season in Boston, Marchand came as advertised and helped the Bruins win their first Stanley Cup since 1972. He had 11 goals in 25 playoff games, a Bruins rookie playoff record, and the team was 9-0 in games that he scored. He had five goals in the last five games against the Vancouver Canucks in the Stanley Cup Final, and he also punched Canucks star Daniel Sedin in the jaw six times when the Bruins had Game 6 in hand. When asked why afterward, he replied, "Because I felt like it."

Marchand was penalized but escaped suspension. He scored two goals in the decisive seventh game, and he's been beloved in Beantown ever since.

In 2015–16 Marchand had 37 goals and a team-leading plus-21 rating. It earned him a spot on Team Canada for the 2016 World Championship, where he won gold. A few months later, he represented his country at the World Cup of Hockey. Playing on Canada's top line, he led the tournament with five goals in six games, including the winning goal in the final, a shorthanded tally with less than a minute remaining.

His confidence buoyed, Marchand challenged for the NHL lead in goals and points in 2016–17, prompting Hart Trophy buzz. He finished tied for fourth in goals (39) and fifth in points (85), both career highs.

Marchand took it to another level in 2018–19, tying Crosby for fifth in scoring at an even 100 points, including a career-high 64 assists. In the playoffs, he equaled Conn Smythe Trophy-winner Ryan O'Reilly for first in playoff scoring with 23 points, but the Bruins lost to the St. Louis Blues in the Stanley Cup Final.

The numbers don't lie. In points or punishment, and both are piling up. Marchand had 80 points in 70 games to lead the Bruins in 2021–22, his sixth straight season at more than a point per game, and his 11 points in Boston's seven-game loss to the Carolina Hurricanes in the first round were tops on the team.

Since 2010–11, Marchand is fifth in the NHL in goals and seventh in points, and he's third in playoff points with 118, just one behind Crosby.

Marchand stands alone in another category. By punching Pittsburgh Penguins goalie Tristan Jarry in the head and then jabbing him in the throat with his stick in a 2022 game, he earned an NHL-record eighth suspension, and he wasn't even disciplined for licking Ryan Callahan in 2018. He's also forfeited more than $1.4 million in salary.

At least Bruins' opponents will have some relief from Marchand early in the 2022–23 season after offseason surgery on both hips, whether he's using his stick for good or evil.

Won gold at the 2007 and 2008 World Junior Championship

Won the Stanley Cup in 2011

Won gold at the 2016 World Championship

Won the World Cup of Hockey in 2016

Played in two NHL All-Star Games (2017, 2018)

MITCHELL MARNER

Maple Leafs | Right Wing | 93

At 16, Marner had 46 assists and 59 points in his first OHL season, but he had a slow start to his draft season of 2014–15. His family brought him home and reminded him to have fun again, and after the reset he had 13 goals and 16 assists in 10 games and finished with 44 goals and 126 points in 62 games.

By the 2015 NHL draft, Hunter was at the helm of the Toronto Maple Leafs as interim GM and didn't hesitate to select the homegrown kid again, this time fourth overall. Toronto then sent Marner back to London for one more season so he could go win everything.

After getting 116 points in 57 regular seasons games in 2015–16 to be named both the OHL's Most Outstanding Player and the CHL's Player of the Year, Marner went supernova in the playoffs. He had 44 points in only 18 games to win OHL playoff MVP for the champion Knights, then he led the Memorial Cup with 14 points and was tournament MVP after London beat the Rouyn-Noranda Huskies 3–2 in overtime.

It was also the year the Leafs had the first over-all pick and drafted Auston Matthews, who would become his friend, linemate, TikTok co-star and fellow Justin Bieber collaborator.

Marner's NHL breakout came in 2018–19 with 68 assists and 94 points, good for 11th in the NHL, and a plus-22 rating. On the back of that season and after a very public negotiation, Toronto signed restricted free agent Marner to a six-year contract worth $10.9 million a year.

Despite an ankle injury early in the season, Marner's 34 assists and 47 points in 38 games earned him a trip to the All-Star Game, and he ended the shortened season with 67 points in 59 games.

Marner had another 67 points in 2020–21, an ominous number for the Maple Leafs, in just 55 games of the pandemic-delayed season. He led the Leafs in scoring and was fourth in the NHL, as Toronto finished first in the realigned North Division.

N ow generously listed at 6-foot-0 and 172 pounds, Mitch Marner was 5-foot-7 and 125 pounds when the London Knights chose him 19th overall in the 2013 OHL draft. The Thornhill, Ontario, native had 86 points in 56 games with the Don Mills Flyers and Knights general manager Mark Hunter, who had 1,426 NHL penalty minutes, saw potential in the little bundle of energy when many others didn't.

"I had a couple coaches tell me when I was younger, 'Have fun playing minor hockey, because that's all you'll ever play,'" said Marner. "That's why I always play like it's my last day."

In the first round of the playoffs, Toronto faced historic rival the Montreal Canadiens, who were a distant fourth, and took a three games to one series lead but let it slip away. Marner had an ill-timed delay of game penalty in Game 6 that cost his team a goal, and when the Leafs lost Game 7, he was a lightning rod for fan dissatisfaction and five-and-a-half decades of Stanley Cup angst.

Marner had only four assists in the series, and just one over the last three games. He had gone 18 playoff games without a goal and had the same number of goals (five) as delay-of-game penalties in his 32 post-season games. For the seventh-highest paid player in the NHL that wasn't enough. Although he'd deleted all social media, the vitriol was impossible to ignore.

It would wilt many players, but Marner showed he's made of sterner stuff in 2021–22. Like his junior draft year, Marner started the season off slowly, earning just one assist in the first seven games, and then suffered a shoulder injury. But he found the fun again.

Marner was tied for 95th in NHL scoring on January 1, 2022, and ended the season 10th. He had career highs with 35 goals and 97 points in 72 games, while also being an elite defender and penalty killer.

Hopes were high after a franchise record 115-point season but dashed again with another first round loss, the Leafs' sixth in a row, this time to the Tampa Bay Lightning in seven games. Marner had three points in Game 1 and two goals and eight points in the series, but only two assists over the last four games.

This time the ire of Leafs Nation was focused elsewhere; they know the future is in the soft hands of the undersized whiz kid with the unbridled enthusiasm and sublime talent. The one who makes everyone he plays with better, notably Hart Trophy winner Matthews.

As James van Riemsdyk said of former linemate Marner: "He was playing chess when everyone else was playing checkers."

Named OHL Most Outstanding Player and CHL Player of the Year in 2015–16	
Memorial Cup leading scorer, MVP and champion in 2016	
Named to the 2016–17 NHL All-Rookie Team	
Played in the 2020 NHL All-Star Game	
NHL First Team All-Star in 2020–21 and 2021–22	

AARON EKBLAD

Panthers | Defense | 5

53 points and 91 penalty minutes in 58 regular season games. He also had seven goals and 17 points in the playoffs, with a plus-11 rating.

With scuttlebutt surrounding Ekblad and the first-overall pick in the upcoming entry draft, the 18-year-old responded with veteran savvy: "I'm a very calm person. It is what it is. It's the NHL draft. We've been preparing for this our whole lives. No one should be nervous here."

With the first pick in 2014, the Florida Panthers knew they had their man after interviewing Ekblad. "He just blew us out of the water, because his professionalism and maturity was incredible," said then-general manager Dale Tallon. "You go, this kid's not 18 years old or 17. He's 35. But he had a sparkle in his eye. He was sure of himself. He was a man-child for me. And I liked it."

Once again Ekblad proved he was worthy. He had 12 goals and 39 points, the third-highest total by an 18-year-old defenseman in league history. He was the first teenage blue-liner in five years to play more than 1,700 minutes, and he became the youngest defenseman to win the Calder Trophy since Orr in 1967.

In his sophomore season, Ekblad played in his second All-Star Game and the Panthers won the Atlantic Division. He signed an eight-year, $60 million contract and was named alternate captain prior to the 2016–17 season, but he got off to a slow start, and the Panthers slid out of playoff contention.

Ekblad suffered the first concussion of his young career, and it followed either a mild concussion or whiplash (depending who you ask) that he sustained when he was playing for Team North America in the 2016 World Cup of Hockey. The Panthers shut him down for the last 14 games, protecting their most valuable asset.

Ekblad didn't miss a game over the next two seasons, then set career highs with 36 assists and 41 points in only 67 games of the pandemic-shortened 2019–20 season. But injuries got him again.

Ekblad was sidelined for the final 21 games of the

Aaron Ekblad has long been exceptional. In 2011, the Ontario Hockey League made it official, granting the 15-year-old Belle River, Ontario, native "Exceptional Player Status" so he could be drafted a year early. Already 6-foot-3 and 200-pounds, he had 34 points in 30 regular season games and 21 points in 18 playoff games for the Sun County Panthers minor midget team.

Ekblad was the first defenseman in the Canadian Hockey League to be given exceptional status, and the grateful Barrie Colts made him the first-overall pick in the OHL draft. It was not a mistake; he won the 2012 Emms Family Award as Rookie of the Year.

In his third and final OHL season, Ekblad was named Most Outstanding Defenseman after 23 goals,

2020–21 season and the playoffs after fracturing his left leg in a gruesome fashion. He returned from that devastating injury to have the best season of his career, but he was forced to sit out the last 20 games of the 2021–22 season with a right leg injury, on the first shift of the game after he become the Panther's all-time leader in points by a defenseman.

At that point Ekblad had set new career highs with 42 assists and 57 points in 61 games, which was fifth in the NHL among defensemen when he was hurt. He finished seventh among defensemen with a plus-38 and a 3.68 Game Score Value Added, while skating 24:55 a night, tops on the Panthers. At season's end, he finished sixth in Norris Trophy voting.

Ekblad's 97 goals and 291 points are Florida franchise records for defensemen, and he's still just 26. He's inching closer to grizzled veteran than child prodigy,

Named OHL Rookie of the Year in 2012
Named the OHL's Most Outstanding Defenseman in 2014
Selected first overall in the 2014 NHL entry draft
Played in two NHL All-Star Games (2015, 2016)
Won the Calder Trophy in 2015

but he's still in his prime years, especially for a blueliner. An uninterrupted season will get him into the Norris Trophy hunt that he was robbed of two years in a row. More importantly, his President's Trophy-winning Panthers have to seize the day while they can after years of playoff disappointment.

As the old soul Ekblad said when addressing student-athletes back in Windsor, Ontario, "Nothing lasts forever. You have to take advantage of what this world has to offer."

MORGAN RIELLY

Maple Leafs | Defense | 44

Morgan Rielly's mother, Shirley, says her son was an average, happy kid who had a good group of friends in his West Vancouver neighborhood. "The difference was that he wanted so desperately to play competitive hockey," she said.

"When Morgan's team went to some tournaments and didn't have great success, the losses would be devastating to him, but he'd also be upset because the losses didn't seem to bother some of his teammates. He wanted to be in an environment where everybody felt the same as he did about winning."

So at 14 Rielly moved to Wilcox, Saskatchewan, to play at hockey factory Notre Dame, where he captained the team to a national title. He then went to Moose Jaw to play for the Warriors, who took him second overall in the Western Hockey League draft in 2009. In his second season, he was ranked as high as second by NHL Central Scouting, but he tore his ACL and played only 18 games.

The Toronto Maple Leafs were undeterred by the injury and took Rielly fifth overall in 2012. Then-general manager Brian Burke couldn't pass up the swift, creative defenseman and said he would have drafted Rielly first overall if he had the pick.

In 2013–14, at 19, Rielly stuck with the Maple Leafs and proved himself mature beyond his years. He played 73 games and was second among rookie defensemen in assists (25) and sixth in points (27).

Expectations were high in Toronto for the 6-foot-1, 221-pound Rielly, and over the course of two more bleak years, he was often the team's best player. Some luck and high picks gave the roster William Nylander, Mitch Marner and Auston Matthews in 2016–17, and suddenly, at 22, Rielly had become a veteran on one of the youngest teams in the NHL.

In March 2017, Rielly turned 23 and played his 300th NHL game, and a few weeks later, the Leafs clinched the first playoff berth of his NHL career.

Their prize was the Washington Capitals, and the young Leafs took them to six games, five of which went to overtime.

"You learn more from the tough times than you do from the good times, and I think it's good to go through these things when you are young," said Rielly. "It's a bit of an eye-opener and it's not all going to be easy."

It certainly hasn't been for Rielly and his team. They have become a regular-season powerhouse but followed that playoff baptism with two more first-round losses, both in seven games to the Boston Bruins.

Rielly, meanwhile, has transformed into one of the team's leaders. When asked about teammate Jake Gardiner, the object of much scorn after the 2019 elimination game, Rielly cursed on Hockey Night in Canada in defense of his fellow defenseman. To stand up for his teammates after a heartbreaking loss is the kind of character that earns respect.

In 2018–19 Rielly led all NHL defensemen with 20 goals and was third among blueliners with 72 points. He's just the third Toronto defenseman to have 70 points in a season, after Borje Salming and Ian Turnbull, and the first to score 20 goals since Al Iafrate in 1989–90.

During the 2019–20 season, Rielly became the second defenseman in franchise history to start his career with seven straight 20-assist seasons, after Salming, and in 2021–22 Rielly set a new career high with 58 assists. That tied him for fifth among defensemen with Norris Trophy-winner Cale Makar, and he tied for sixth with 68 points, while also adding penalty-killing duties to his repertoire. He now has two of the eight highest-scoring seasons by a defenseman in franchise history.

Rielly signed an eight-year, $60-million contract extension in 2021, and if he stays healthy, he has a

shot at becoming the Leafs' all-time leader in games played and passing Salming to be first in scoring by defensemen.

A playoff series victory is Rielly's first priority, however. In 2022 Toronto was out in the first round yet again, this time to the two-time defending champion Tampa Bay Lightning. It was the sixth straight year exiting at the first opportunity.

The longest-serving member on the current roster was the first to face the media after the 2-1 Game 7 loss in 2022. Rielly had the goal, one of three to go with three assists he had in the series. A burning desire to win and accountability when his team doesn't is why management committed long-term.

His teammates were unanimous in their support. As Hart Trophy-winner Matthews put it: "His voice carries a lot of weight in the room, and we all look up to him."

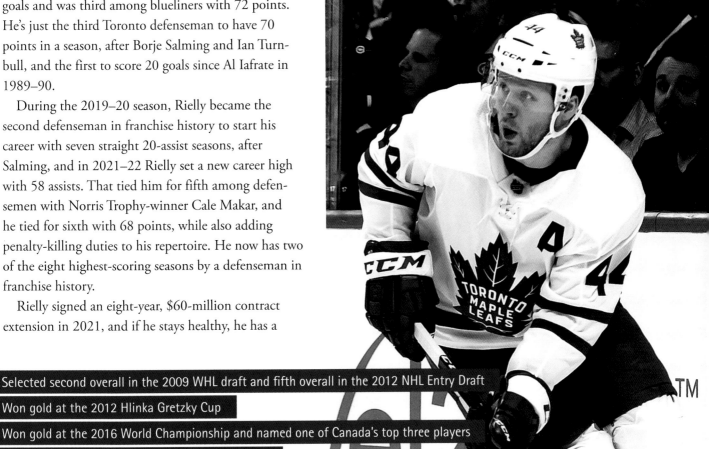

Selected second overall in the 2009 WHL draft and fifth overall in the 2012 NHL Entry Draft

Won gold at the 2012 Hlinka Gretzky Cup

Won gold at the 2016 World Championship and named one of Canada's top three players

Led all NHL defensemen with 20 goals in 2018–19

CAREY PRICE

Carey Price grew up in Anahim Lake, a remote town in central British Columbia. He has Nuxalk and Southern Carrier Indigenous heritage, and his mother, Lynda, is the former chief of the Ulkatcho First Nation and the first woman elected to the Union of BC Indian Chiefs' board of directors.

The goaltending genes came from his father, Jerry, an eighth-round pick of the Philadelphia Flyers in 1978 whose bad knees kept him from reaching the NHL. There were no rinks in Anahim Lake, so Jerry cleared a section of Corkscrew Creek.

At 9, Carey had outgrown the creek, but the closest team was in Williams Lake, 200 miles away. After making the eight-hour round trip too many times, his father bought a small plane to shorten the commute.

The seventh overall pick in the 2002 Western Hockey League draft by the Tri-City Americans, Price went fifth overall in the 2005 NHL draft, despite the Montreal Canadiens having a Vezina and Hart Trophy winner in Jose Theodore. Then-general manager Bob Gainey couldn't pass up a "thoroughbred."

After the Americans were eliminated in the 2007 WHL playoffs, Price joined Hamilton for the American Hockey League postseason and posted a .936 save percentage to lead the Bulldogs to the Calder Cup. It topped a season in which he'd also won gold at the 2007 World Junior Championship. He was the first goalie to be named Canadian Hockey League Goaltender of the Year, World Juniors MVP and AHL playoff MVP in the same season.

Unflappable under brighter spotlights at the 2014 Sochi Olympics, Price had a 0.59 goals-against average and .972 save percentage in five games, all victories, which included a shutout streak of 164:19 that stretched over the semifinal and gold medal game.

That was merely a prelude to a historic 2014–15 season. Price's league-leading 44 wins broke the franchise record, and he was first in goals-against average (1.96) and save percentage (.933). He won the Hart Trophy, Vezina Trophy and Ted Lindsay Award, and shared the William Jennings Trophy.

During an acceptance speech, Price said, "I would really like to encourage First Nations youth to be leaders in their communities. Be proud of your heritage and don't be discouraged from the improbable."

Price signed a record eight-year, $84 million contract in 2017, and after passing Jacques Plante for the most wins in Canadiens' history with his 315th in March 2019, he again proved his worth when it matters most.

The Canadiens made the qualifying round of the shortened 2019–20 season as the lowest ranked team, but upset the Pittsburgh Penguins before falling in the second round. Price was first in the playoffs in both goals-against average (1.78) and save percentage (.936).

A year later, with play that inspires confidence in teammates and robs opponents of it, Price led Montreal to a comeback victory over the heavily favored Toronto Maple Leafs in the North Division after being down three games to one. He then carried the underdogs to wins over the Winnipeg Jets and Vegas Golden Knights for an improbable and thrilling run to the Stanley Cup Final as the rapturous city emerged from pandemic lockdowns. It ended against the Tampa Bay Lightning, who won their second Cup in a row, and Price finished with a .924 save percentage and 2.28 goals-against average.

These playoffs took a toll on Price. He had offseason knee surgery, and on the eve of the 2021–22 season,

he checked himself into the NHL's player assistance program.

Intensely proud and private, Price released a statement after he'd completed substance abuse treatment. "Over the last few years, I have let myself get to a very dark place and I didn't have the tools to cope with that struggle," he wrote. "Asking for help when you need it is what we encourage our kids to do. And it was what I needed to do."

Price was voted the winner of the 2022 Bill Masterton Trophy for "perseverance, sportsmanship and dedication to hockey" despite playing only five games at the tail end of the season.

Price made his 700th career start and earned his 361st win days after the Canadiens lost franchise icon Guy Lafleur in April 2022. The one player from the 21st century who joins Lafleur in that pantheon, Price's future remains murky with continued knee problems and a new regime rebuilding the team.

When Price does choose to walk away, a place in the Bell Centre rafters and Hall of Fame assured, he'll do it the same way he played. On his own terms.

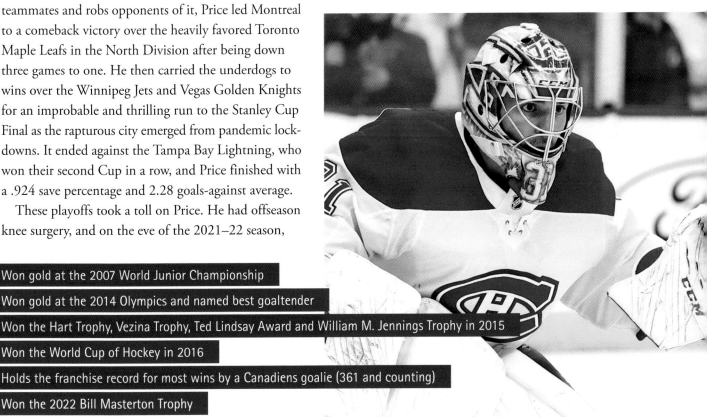

Won gold at the 2007 World Junior Championship

Won gold at the 2014 Olympics and named best goaltender

Won the Hart Trophy, Vezina Trophy, Ted Lindsay Award and William M. Jennings Trophy in 2015

Won the World Cup of Hockey in 2016

Holds the franchise record for most wins by a Canadiens goalie (361 and counting)

Won the 2022 Bill Masterton Trophy

DYLAN LARKIN

Red Wings | Center | 71

The Township of Waterford, Michigan, is about 35 miles northwest of Detroit's Little Caesars Arena. Calling itself Lakeland Paradise, it's a shinny player's dream, with 35 lakes for 75,000 citizens. It's where Hall of Famer Pat LaFontaine grew up and where Dylan Larkin cut his hockey teeth.

"Just me and a puck and a net," remembered Larkin. "That was my childhood. Up here [in the NHL], you want to put up points and win, but there it's just about hockey."

After Larkin's 17 goals and 26 points in 26 games during his second season with the U.S. National Team Development Program, the Red Wings made the local kid the 15th overall pick in 2014, their highest selection since 1991, a reflection of the team's success.

Larkin had 15 goals and 47 points in 35 games for the University of Michigan in 2014–15 and was named the Big Ten freshman of the year. He had impressed Team USA brass at the 2015 World Juniors earlier in the year, so after his only season as a Wolverine, he was added to the U.S. roster at the World Championship and the 19-year-old helped the Americans win bronze.

Not done yet, Larkin joined the Grand Rapids Griffins, Detroit's American Hockey League affiliate, midway through the playoffs and had three goals and five points in six games — his only stint in the minors.

The Red Wings have a history of bringing young players along slowly, but Larkin forced them to make an exception. He had a goal and an assist in his NHL debut in 2015–16, making him the first teen to score for the team since Red Wings legend and general manager Steve Yzerman in 1983.

Larkin had 23 goals and 45 points in his rookie year and made the 2016 NHL All-Star Game, where he set a record for fastest skater at 13.172 seconds around the rink in the skills competition.

In 2016–17 the Red Wings failed to qualify for the postseason for the first time in 25 straight seasons, but it allowed Larkin to play at the 2017 World Championship, where he had 10 points in eight games.

Moving from Henrik Zetterberg's wing to center, Larkin set career highs with 47 assists and 63 points in 2017–18. When Zetterberg retired at the end of the season Larkin took over as the team's number one center and continued his ascent to elite status. His 73 points in 2018–19 tied his friend and former USNTDP teammate Auston Matthews of the Toronto Maple Leafs. He played in all situations and was ninth among all NHL forwards in ice time at 21:51.

Larkin also achieved the exceedingly rare trifecta of leading his team in goals (32), assists (41) and penalty minutes (75). Although there's scant record of Gordie

Howe actually doing this, having a goal, an assist and a fight in one game became known as the "Gordie Howe hat trick." It's a nod to the Red Wing legend's multi-faceted game and history of stuffing the whole stat sheet. Detroit fans had witnessed the birth of the Dylan Larkin hat trick, the modern season-long equivalent in which pugilism has been replaced with penalty minutes.

Larkin led the team again in assists (34) and points (53) in the shortened 2019–20 season, and he was named team captain in January 2021, the first since Zetterberg retired in 2018 and just the fourth in 34 years. He joined the elite company of Yzerman (1986–2006) and Niklas Lidstrom (2006–2012), two of the 13 Red Wings captains now in the Hall of Fame.

"I think I understand the significance of this role. I've seen it my whole life, been a fan, been around fans, been to games, to know what it means to not only be a Detroit Red Wing, but to now be the captain," said Larkin. "I couldn't be more honored."

The leader was back on top of the Wings' chart in 2021–22 in goals (31) and points (69) and was second in assists (38). He played in the All-Star Game and was on his way to career highs in all three categories when core muscle surgery ended his season at 71 games.

Larkin still has a healthy penalty minute tally — 327 career and counting — but he's ceded that statistical category to teammates. After not making the playoffs since his rookie year and in his prime, he's more concerned about getting some postseason points and wins, and that's what he told his young teammates.

"As the captain of the team, my message to guys was 'You got your feet wet, but next year it's time to take this thing over.'"

Won gold at the 2014 Under-18 World Championship
Won bronze at the 2015 and 2018 World Championships
Set a record for fastest skater at the 2016 NHL All-Star Game Skills Competition
Played in two NHL All-Star Games (2016, 2022)

DAVID PASTRNAK

Bruins | Right Wing | 88

Before David Pastrnak left his hometown of Havirov, Czech Republic, to play hockey in Sweden, he asked his father, Milan, a former professional hockey player and coach for a workout regime. Milan had wanted to keep hockey out of their relationship, so he told his son he'd only help when asked. The exercise plan was so tough that it was abandoned shortly after.

At 16, Pastrnak was off to Sodertalje to play for the same team that Los Angeles Kings captain Anze Kopitar had joined to develop his game. While he was there, Milan succumbed to cancer.

"The only place I wasn't thinking about it was the rink," said Pastrnak. "Every time I went home I was there by myself. The walls were empty, I couldn't call my mom 24-7. So I think I spent around six, seven hours a day at the rink."

The extra work paid off. Pastrnak was a highly rated NHL prospect who impressed a Gretzky at a pre-draft dinners. "He had a lot of life to him, and you just really hoped the best for him," said Keith Gretzky, the Boston Bruins director of amateur scouting at the time. "All three of us walked away going, boy, we really hope that he's a guy who plays in the NHL one day and that if it's not for us, then it's for somebody else."

There were some who questioned whether the skinny kid could withstand the rigors of North American hockey, but when Pastrnak was still available, the Bruins happily selected him with the 25th overall pick in the 2014 draft. After his name was announced, he hugged his mother, Marcela, and pointed to the sky. The NHL dream he shared with his father had come true.

Pastrnak began the 2014–15 season in the American Hockey League with the Providence Bruins, but after getting 28 points in his first 25 games, he was called up. He finished the season with 27 points in 46 NHL games.

"You look at the core strength from the first year to the second year to the third year, he paid the price," according to Gretzky.

In his third season, Pastrnak broke out, opening the season with 18 goals in 23 games and ending it second on the team with 70 points in 2016–17.

Pastrnak signed a six-year, $40 million contract before the 2017–18 season and then led the team with 35 goals and finished second with 80 points. It was also the birth of what became known as the "Perfection Line," with Pastrnak and Brad Marchand flanking Patrice Bergeron.

In the 2018 playoffs, Pastrnak flew out of the gate with nine points in the first two games against the Toronto Maple Leafs to tie a postseason record, including three goals and three assists in Game 2. The Bruins fell to the Tampa Bay Lightning in round two, but Pastrnak had 20 points in 12 postseason games.

A thumb injury sidelined Pastrnak in 2018–19, but he still had 38 goals and 81 points in 66 games. Back for the playoffs, he had nine goals and 10 assists in 24 games to help the Bruins reach the Stanley Cup Final.

In 2019–20, Pastrnak tied for third in the NHL with 95 points and shared the Maurice Richard Trophy with Alex Ovechkin after they each had 48 goals. The Atlantic Division captain at the All-Star Game was robbed of the magical 50-goal mark by COVID-19.

At the end of the 2021–22 season, Pastrnak had 240 goals and 504 points in 510 games played. Only Bobby Orr and Ray Bourque reached the 500-point milestone faster in franchise history. He's second in his draft year in goals, assists and points, and ninth among all players in goals scored since he entered the league.

Pastrnak does it on the international stage too. He tied for first at the 2022 World Championship with seven goals, including a hat trick in the third period to beat Team USA in the bronze medal match and win Czechia's first medal in a decade.

But not all was well back in Beantown. Bruce Cassidy, his first coach in Providence, was fired and Bergeron was pondering retirement. Close friends Torey Krug and David Krejci, who put Pastrnak up when he moved to Boston, were let go in recent seasons.

It all means that Pastrnak staying in Boston beyond the final year of his contract in 2022–23 is no sure thing. As Gretzky said, "family means everything to him," and the Bruins have become a little dysfunctional.

Led the NHL with 10 game-winning goals and won the Maurice Richard Trophy in 2019–20 (shared with Alex Ovechkin)

Played in two NHL All-Star Games (2019, 2020)

Broke Jaromir Jagr's record of four consecutive "Golden Hockey Sticks" as Czech Player of the Year with his fifth straight in 2021

Tied for first in goals (7) the 2022 World Championship and won bronze

ALEKSANDER BARKOV

Panthers | Center | 16

Aleksander Barkov was 29 when he left his home in the former Soviet Union to go to Tampere, Finland, to play for Tappara. It's where his son, Aleksander, was born and where the younger Barkov made his professional debut on October 1, 2011, at the age of 16 years and 29 days old and became the youngest player in Liiga history to earn a point. A few months later, he became the youngest player to wear a Finland sweater at the World Juniors and the youngest Finn to score a goal at the tournament.

In the second of his two seasons with Tappara's senior team, Barkov had 48 points in 53 games. He finished ninth in league scoring, one spot behind teammate and former NHLer Ville Nieminen, another Tampere native. Nieminen played alongside father and son on Tappara and says Aleksander got the best of both Russian and Finnish hockey.

"Everything looked professional," said Nieminen. "All his moves, hockey IQ. He's the best student of the game I've ever seen."

The Florida Panthers saw it too and made Barkov the second overall selection behind Nathan MacKinnon in the 2013 NHL draft, ahead of Seth Jones, who was widely assumed to be the number two pick.

It was an unexpected and prescient move, and once again Barkov set the bar for precociousness. He made his NHL debut on October 3, 2013, at the age of 18 years and 31 days old, and became the youngest player to score an NHL goal since Don Raleigh of the New York Rangers in 1943.

Barkov's rookie season was derailed by a knee injury he sustained at the 2014 Olympics, which cost him 24 games. The injury bug continued to bite him over the next three seasons, as back, hand and wrist injuries knocked him out of the lineup for a total of 48 games.

Barkov finally had a healthy season in 2017–18, and it showed on the scoresheet as well as in league-wide recognition. He had 27 goals and 78 points in 79 games, played in the All-Star Game and led the NHL with five shorthanded goals. He finished third in voting for the Lady Byng Trophy and fourth for the Frank J. Selke Trophy.

Just prior to the 2018–19 season, two weeks after turning 23, the 6-foot-3, 213-pound centerman was named captain of the Panthers. "He has all of the qualities of a great leader," said then-general manager Dale Tallon. "Unrivaled work ethic, wisdom beyond his years and the respect and admiration of his teammates. Aleksander's determination and passion for the game have made him one of the NHL's best and most complete players."

It proved to be another wise choice by the Panthers. Barkov finished 10th in the NHL with 96 points, and he scored one of the highlights of the NHL season: a between-the-legs top-shelf goal that was part of a hat trick against the Montreal Canadiens.

Playing all 82 games, Barkov broke Pavel Bure's 19-year-old franchise record for points in a season and won the Lady Byng after taking only eight minutes in penalties.

In 2020–21 Barkov added his first Selke Trophy after leading the Panthers with 26 goals in 50 games and helping Florida to its best-ever points percentage (.705). He also led Florida forwards in takeaways (39) and average ice time (20:56), and set personal highs in face-off winning percentage (54.9) and shot attempts percentage (58.6).

The following season Barkov lost time to a knee injury and his single-season scoring record to friend, occasional linemate, alternate captain, and the only player who'd been on the team longer before his trade to Calgary, Jonathan Huberdeau, who had 115 points. Barkov had 88 points in 67 games and passed Olli Jokinen to become the franchise leader in career goals, as the two led the Panthers to their first President's Trophy.

Playoff hopes were high in 2022, but after

eliminating the Washington Capitals in six games, the Panthers' first series win since their trip to the Stanley Cup Final in 1996, the two-time defending champion Tampa Bay Lightning beat them in the second Battle of Florida in two years.

Barkov signed an eight-year, $80 million contract extension prior to the season, and the 27-year-old has plenty of time to chase down Huberdeau for the franchise records in games played, assists and points, not to mention the biggest trophy of them all.

"I have two homes now, one in Finland, in Tampere. And one here," said Barkov when he signed. And he's become kind of a big deal there.

"I was going to Miami yesterday, and I saw myself two or three times on the billboard. I'm not going to lie. It's amazing. But it doesn't affect me in any way. I gotta still work. It's not going to be there forever."

| Won bronze at the 2014 Olympics |
| Won silver at the 2016 World Championship |
| Played in the 2018 NHL All-Star Game |
| Won the Lady Byng Trophy in 2019 |
| Won the Selke Trophy in 2021 |

THOMAS CHABOT

Senators | Defense | 72

At the 2017 World Juniors, Chabot led all defensemen in goals (four) and points (10) and all players in average ice time (26:14). He was named the tournament's best defenseman and won the MVP award, the first blue-liner ever.

Despite losing to Team USA in a shootout for the gold, Canada's alternate captain was the player of the game after skating for 43:53 minutes, including 11:06 in the 20-minute overtime, with a goal and an assist.

"He was great, he was dominant," said head coach Dominique Ducharme. "He was good offensively and defensively, shutting down the best players on the other side. He was just tremendous all tournament."

Chabot finished the 2016–17 QMJHL season with 45 points in 34 games, matching his point total from the year prior in 13 fewer games and becoming the Sea Dogs' all-time leading scorer among defensemen. He was named QMJHL Personality of the Year, QMJHL Defenseman of the Year and Canadian Hockey League Defenseman of the Year.

The Sea Dogs won the 2017 league championship, and Chabot was awarded playoff MVP after earning 18 assists and 23 points in 18 games and leading all players with a plus-29.

In 2017–18 Chabot played 63 NHL games and had nine goals and 25 points, good for second among NHL rookie defensemen in goals and fifth in points.

Playing with two-time Norris Trophy winner Karlsson accelerated Chabot's development, and he was ready to take over as the team's top rearguard when Karlsson was traded to the San Jose Sharks in 2018. Chabot let that be known in the second game of the year with a two-goal, three-point effort against the Toronto Maple Leafs, including a dangle and finish worthy of the most offensively gifted forwards.

Chabot had 10 goals and 38 points through the first 38 games of the season, second among NHL defensemen, when he suffered a shoulder injury. A broken

Losing all-world defenseman Erik Karlsson in the Senators' 2018 fire sale was a blow to the team's blue line and fan base, but there was a worthy successor on the roster, waiting just to his left.

Thomas Chabot grew up in Sainte-Marie, Quebec. He spoke only French when he was picked by the Quebec Major Junior Hockey League's Sea Dogs in anglophone Saint John, New Brunswick, but he quickly adapted and became one of the city's favorite sons.

The Senators took him 18th overall in the 2015 draft, and Chabot made his NHL debut in 2016. He played just one game before being sent back to Saint John for the remainder of the 2016–17 season. Instead of sulking, he had 15 points in his first 10 games and then lit the junior hockey world on fire.

toe later in the season also forced him to sit out, but he finished with 41 assists and 55 points in 70 games, putting him 10th among NHL defensemen. Chabot also averaged 24:17 of ice time, just ahead of Norris Trophy winner Mark Giordano, and was fifth in the NHL with 20:45 at even strength.

Ice time is an indicator of a coach's faith, fitness, responsibility on the penalty kill and flair for the power play. Chabot has it all and makes it look smooth and effortless. In 2019–20 he led the NHL with 26:00 minutes a game and was second in 2020–21 and again in 2021–22.

Chabot was limited to 59 games in 2021–22 and a broken hand in March looked like it ended his season, but he returned for the last four games of the season and was named Captain Canada for the World Championship. Canada lost the gold medal game in overtime to host Finland with Chabot in the penalty box for a questionable call.

There was a silver lining to that loss for Canada, as Chabot hopes for the nation's capital after another year on the outside looking in. Named Ottawa's alternate captain in 2021, he had an "honest" conversation

Won silver and named top defenseman and tournament MVP at the 2017 World Junior Championship	
Won the QMJHL's Emile "Butch" Bouchard Trophy as best defenseman and named CHL Defenseman of the Year in 2017	
Named QMJHL playoff MVP in 2017	
Played in the 2019 NHL All-Star Game	
Led the NHL in average ice time in 2019–20 (26:00)	
Won silver at the 2019 and 2022 World Championships	
Captain of Team Canada at the 2022 World Championship	

about the state of the Senators, according to general manager Pierre Dorion.

There are talented young players in place and the team had streaks of brilliance, but Chabot, who is signed until 2028, has yet to taste the postseason. "Everybody has taken a step and everybody has improved, but I think for us as players, I think it's time for us to start winning and start bringing this team to a whole other level," he said.

Chabot has grown into a leadership role and he's not afraid to use his voice, in either official language.

RASMUS DAHLIN

Sabres | Defense | 26

Rasmus Dahlin was born in Lidkoping and grew up in Trollhattan, Sweden, where he was playing bandy if he wasn't playing hockey. The former was just as popular, but the latter was in the genes. His father, Martin, was a defenseman in Sweden's lower tiers, and his brother, Felix, played professionally until he was forced to retire at 20 because of arthritis. The condition also affects his mother and sister but skipped Rasmus.

Growing up Dahlin played forward, and his favorite player was Peter Forsberg. But when he was 13 it dawned on him that if he played defense he could be on the ice for half the game and dictate the offense from the back.

It was a smart move. Just three years later, Dahlin joined Frolunda at the top of the Swedish Hockey League for the 2016–17 season.

"I never played with or against a defenseman who has anything close to his ability to read the play out there and his sense of time and space. I'm not talking about young defensemen. I'm talking any defenseman. His skating is off the charts. So are his skills," said Frolunda teammate Jonathan Sigalet.

Mid-season, and still just 16, Dahlin played in his first World Juniors, and a year later he truly made a name for himself at the tournament. He was named the top defenseman in Buffalo in 2018, and after a loss to Canada in the gold medal game, he was promptly suspended for two games by the International Ice Hockey Federation for taking his silver medal off during the ceremony. It was part youthful petulance, part competitive passion and something he learned from his idol.

"He's a little like a Peter Forsberg character," according to Team Sweden coach Tomas Monten. "He gets really mean. He has a high temper. That gives him a competitive edge at practices and especially in games. He doesn't lose his head, but he competes."

About six weeks later, Dahlin made his Olympic debut for Sweden in PyeongChang, South Korea. At 17 years old, he was the team's youngest player by seven years and the first to go from the World Juniors to the Olympics since Hall of Famer Eric Lindros did so with Canada in 1992.

When the Buffalo Sabres surprised no one and chose Dahlin with the team's first number one overall selection since 1987, he became the first Swede at the top of the draft since Mats Sundin in 1989 and only the third defenseman picked first overall in 22 seasons.

Dahlin played all 82 games in 2018–19 and finished second in assists (35) and third in points (44) among all rookies. He was just the third defenseman in NHL history with 40-plus points when starting the season as an 18-year-old, surpassing Bobby Orr's 41 points and second only to the 66 points earned by former Sabre and his first NHL coach, Phil Housley.

After two seasons, Dahlin had 84 points (13 goals, 71 assists), second-most in NHL history by a defenseman before turning 20, again behind Hall of Famer Housley, and that included a pandemic-shortened season.

The 2020–21 season was one to forget, for both Dahlin and the Sabres, who suffered through an 18-game losing streak. But there were plenty of signs of hope when the league returned to the regular divisions and number of games.

In 2021–22 Dahlin career highs in goals (13), assists (40), points (53) and average ice time (24:01). He was the first Sabres defenseman with 50 points since 1995–96, and he has two of the three most productive seasons by a Buffalo defenseman in the last 25 years with his .678 and .663 points per game in 2019–20 and 2021–22.

Dahlin was 10th among NHL defensemen in goals and 13th in points in 2021–22 and played in his first All-Star Game, but that wasn't enough for him: "I'm not satisfied. This is the year I'm starting to play against the other team's top line and trying to figure out how to play. I just want to take steps in all the areas. I want to be a defenseman that the coaches can trust in every single situation.

"So, I think I want to say I have a lot more to give."

Won the European Champions League with Frolunda in 2017

Won silver and named best defenseman at the 2018 World Junior Championship

Named Swedish Junior Player of the Year in 2018, the first 17-year-old to win it since 1984

Selected first overall in the 2018 NHL Entry Draft

Voted a finalist for the Calder Trophy in 2019

Played in the 2022 All-Star Game

SERGEI BOBROVSKY

Panthers | Goalie | 72

As an undrafted free agent, Sergei Bobrovsky rose from obscurity to become a Vezina Trophy winner in 2013. But by 2015–16, Bobrovsky had fallen on hard times, plagued by groin injuries that robbed him of his swagger.

Bobrovsky is a gym rat, not always a common trait among the goalie fraternity, but the extra weight that he carried in muscle was working against him. So prior to the 2016–17 season, he dropped about 15 pounds.

"You look at his body last year and the body composition, and all his body fats and all that, you'd say it was impossible," said Blue Jackets general manager Jarmo Kekalainen. "That just tells you about his dedication and how serious he is about his professionalism and how he approaches every day."

Having grown up in Siberia, Bobrovsky comes by his work ethic honestly. His father was a coal miner, and his mother worked on the line at a steel factory.

Bobrovsky spent three seasons with his hometown Metallurg Novokuznetsk in the Kontinental Hockey League before the Philadelphia Flyers offered him a contract in 2010. He made his NHL debut in Philly's first game of 2010–11, becoming the youngest goalie in Flyers history to start a season. But the city and franchise have a way of chewing up and spitting out goaltenders, and Bobrovsky lasted only two years before being traded to the Blue Jackets in 2012.

It paid immediate dividends in Ohio. Bobrovsky won the Vezina in the lockout-shortened 2012–13 season and finished fifth in Hart Trophy voting.

In 2014 Bobrovsky returned home to represent Russia at the Sochi Olympics, a disappointing showing for the host country. There was, however, redemption for Russia at the 2014 World Championship, as Bobrovsky finished tops in both goals-against average (1.13) and save percentage (.950) to lead the team to gold.

After revamping his off-season training regimen, a newly lean and flexible Bobrovsky shut out Finland to send Russia to the semifinals of the 2016 World Cup of Hockey. He stopped 91 of 96 shots in the tournament and stood on his head in the semis against eventual champion Canada, with 42 saves.

"Bob" had been put back together again, in mind and body, and his 2.06 goals-against average and .931 save percentage in 2016–17 both led the NHL. He had a career-high 41 wins and won the Vezina for the second time, and the Blue Jackets were the NHL's biggest surprise, finishing fourth overall, up from 27th the year before.

By 2018–19 Bobrovsky was in the final year of his contract and was set to leave Columbus as an unrestricted free agent at season's end. As the trade deadline

approached, Kekalainen resisted the urge to deal his star goalie. Bobrovsky went 11-5 down the stretch to help Columbus to a wild-card berth and finished the season first in the NHL in shutouts (nine) and second in wins (37).

Bobrovsky had a middling playoff history but gave Columbus a farewell gift and increased his own stock with the first series victory in franchise history. He allowed just eight goals in a first-round sweep of the President's Trophy-winning Tampa Bay Lightning. It was the last series Tampa would lose for three years.

The free agent signed a seven-year, $70 million contract with the Panthers but Bobrovsky didn't live up to it in his first two seasons in Florida. His third was his best, and he credited the birth of his daughter on the eve of the season for the turnaround: "You kind of look at life with a different perspective and you appreciate the different things and you become a deeper human."

Bobrovsky started the season 6-0-0, with a .944 save percentage and a 1.88 goals-against average, and finished with a 39-7-3 record. He was tied for first in wins with all-world Andrei Vasilevskiy and three ahead of Vezina Trophy-winner Igor Shesterkin, as the Panthers won the President's Trophy.

His numbers were slightly down in the playoffs but Bobrovsky helped the Panthers to their first playoff series victory since 1996 before falling to Vasilevskiy and the Lightning in round two.

Up against the salary cap, Panthers general manager Bill Zito has to decide if he can afford Bobrovsky, who has a full no-movement clause. It would be big loss for Florida if he agrees to a trade, and not just because of his bounce back season.

Bobrovsky's 336 wins since he entered the league are second to Marc-Andre Fleury's 372, and he had an assist that didn't show up on the scoresheet. After a disappointing season was paused for the pandemic in 2020, he pledged $100,000 to pay arena staff salaries, while also helping secure N95 masks for frontline workers.

Sometimes the true measure of a player's value goes beyond the bottom line.

Won the Vezina Trophy twice (2013, 2017)	
Won gold at the 2014 World Championship	
Named to two NHL All-Star Games (2015, 2017)	
Led the NHL in goals-against average (2.06) and save percentage (.931) in 2016–17	
Led the NHL in shutouts in 2018–19 with nine	
Tied for the NHL lead with 39 wins in 2021–22	

METROPOLITAN DIVISION

FIRST TEAM

46	**SIDNEY CROSBY**	Penguins	Center
48	**ALEXANDER OVECHKIN**	Capitals	Left Wing
50	**ARTEMI PANARIN**	Rangers	Left Wing
52	**ADAM FOX**	Rangers	Defense
54	**KRIS LETANG**	Penguins	Defense
56	**IGOR SHESTERKIN**	Rangers	Goalie

SECOND TEAM

58	**SEBASTIAN AHO**	Hurricanes	Center
60	**EVGENI MALKIN**	Penguins	Center
62	**MIKA ZIBANEJAD**	Rangers	Center
64	**JOHN CARLSON**	Capitals	Defense
66	**ZACH WERENSKI**	Blue Jackets	Defense
68	**FREDERIK ANDERSEN**	Hurricanes	Goalie

TAXI SQUAD

70	**MATHEW BARZAL**	Islanders	Center
72	**SEAN COUTURIER**	Flyers	Center
74	**CHRIS KREIDER**	Rangers	Left Wing
76	**DOUGIE HAMILTON**	Devils	Defense
78	**JACCOB SLAVIN**	Hurricanes	Defense
80	**TRISTAN JARRY**	Penguins	Goalie

SIDNEY CROSBY

Penguins | Center | 87

The mythology has been established — from the dryer in the family basement to the Great One dubbing him "the Next Big Thing," to the Golden Goal — and the legend only grows.

At the age of 7, Sidney Crosby was "head and shoulders above everyone else his age," according to his hockey camp instructor and future Conn Smythe Trophy-winner Brad Richards.

Sid the Kid was 16 when Wayne Gretzky was asked if anyone could break his NHL records. "Yes, Sidney Crosby. He's the best player I've seen since Mario [Lemieux]." Lemieux became Crosby's teammate,

mentor, landlord and boss with the Pittsburgh Penguins, who drafted him first overall in 2005 after he led the Canadian Hockey League in scoring and won CHL Player of the Year twice in a row.

Entering the NHL the same year as Alex Ovechkin, Crosby had 102 points — the youngest player in history with over 100 — but lost the 2006 Calder Trophy to Ovechkin, who had 106.

In their sophomore seasons, Crosby topped Ovi with 120 points to win both the 2007 Art Ross and Hart trophies. He was the second-youngest MVP in NHL history, behind Gretzky, and the youngest scoring champion in major professional sports history. Named captain in 2007, the youngest in NHL history at the time, Crosby also became the youngest captain to lift the Stanley Cup in 2009.

With the 2010 Olympics on home soil, Canadians put their hopes on Crosby's 22-year-old shoulders. He had a quiet tournament until the gold medal game when Crosby took a pass from Jarome Iginla and swept it between Ryan Miller's legs at 7:40 of overtime to give Canada a 3–2 victory over the U.S. Crosby has also won gold at the 2005 World Juniors, the 2014 Olympics, the 2015 World Championship and the 2016 World Cup of Hockey.

Through fate and scheduling Sid and Ovi remain tied together. On January 11, 2017, Ovechkin earned his 1,000th NHL point, against the Penguins, naturally. Five days later they played again and No. 87 — who was born on August 7, 1987 (8/7/87) — had a goal and three assists in an 8–7 win over the Capitals to tie him for 87th on the NHL's all-time scoring list.

A month later Crosby became the 11th youngest player with 1,000 career points, despite missing the equivalent of more than a full season due to serious concussion issues. Reaching it in 757 games he trailed only Gretzky, Lemieux, Bobby Orr and Mike Bossy on the career points-per-game list.

After winning the Stanley Cup in 2016 the Penguins

repeated as champions in 2017. They became the first back-to-back winners in the 21st century, the first in the salary cap era and the first playing with a defense corps that hadn't received one Norris Trophy vote in their collective careers. Crosby won his second straight Conn Smythe — the third player in history to do so and first since Lemieux in 1991 and 1992.

In 2018–19 Crosby had his ninth season of 30-plus goals and his sixth 100-point season. It was his first time hitting the century mark since 2013–14, and only Gretzky, Lemieux, Marcel Dionne, Bossy and Peter Stastny have more. It was also the ninth time he finished top five in points.

After three seasons shortened by COVID and injury, Crosby was one point behind Ovechkin for the active career leader (1,410 to 1,409) in 166 fewer games played at the end of the 2021–22 season — 1.27 points-per-game for Crosby to Ovechkin's 1.11. In the postseason, Crosby's 71 goals are one behind Ovechkin, and he's first in assists (130) and points (201) since 2005–06, 21 points ahead of teammate Evgeni Malkin in second and 60 more than Ovechkin.

Won both the Art Ross Trophy and Hart Trophy in 2007 and 2014
Won the Ted Lindsay Award three times (2007, 2013, 2014)
Won the Stanley Cup three times (2009, 2016, 2017) and the Conn Smythe Trophy twice (2016, 2017)
Won two Olympic golds (2010, 2014)
Won the Maurice Richard Trophy twice (2010, 2017)

The 2022 playoffs were a microcosm for Crosby. He had eight assists and 10 points in six games against the New York Rangers, with former NHL player and ESPN analyst Dominic Moore calling him "the best skilled grinder ever, basically," and noting that he thrives on contact and in tight areas. But that led to another head injury after a long history of concussions, which may have been the difference in the Penguins' seven game loss in round one. It can be tough to watch happen to one of the best hockey minds in the history of the game.

Crosby has three years left on a bargain contract at, yes, $8.7 million a year, and his rare combination of tireless work ethic, fierce competitiveness and otherworldly talent should be appreciated while it lasts. Legends endure, but even Crosby is mortal.

ALEXANDER OVECHKIN

Capitals | Left Wing | 8

One of hockey's enduring clichés is that it's a game of inches. For Alex Ovechkin the perception of his career almost came down to roughly the width of the shaft on a goalie stick.

Down 1–0 in Game 7 of the second round in the 2017 playoffs, the Washington Capitals captain was alone in the slot for a one-timer that was headed for the top corner and a tie, until the smallest part of Marc-Andre Fleury's goalie equipment intervened. Maybe the Capitals wouldn't have beaten the Pittsburgh Penguins anyway, but it fed into the narrative that Ovechkin disappears in the biggest games.

Ovechkin was selected first overall in 2004, and Sidney Crosby was the top pick in 2005 by the Penguins. After the 2004–05 lockout, they made their NHL debuts in 2005–06, and they've been compared ever since.

In his first NHL game, Ovechkin scored twice and hit an opponent so hard that a partition broke. "Within a week or so we knew that we had a real special human being here," said Glen Hanlon, Ovechkin's first NHL coach.

Later in the season Ovechkin showed the rest of the world. Facing the Phoenix Coyotes on January 16, 2006, Ovechkin was knocked down and sliding on his back but somehow managed to hook the puck past a stunned Brian Boucher in goal. It was the highlight of the decade, now simply called The Goal.

A decade later, on January 10, 2016, Ovechkin became the fifth-fastest player to reach 500 goals, and a year and a day after that he scored 35 seconds into a game against the Penguins to earn his 1,000th point in his 880th game. He was the fastest active player to reach the milestone until Crosby bested him a month later, and they're one-two in points since they entered the league, separated by a single point at the end of 2021–22 — 1,410 for Ovechkin and 1,409 for Crosby.

Ovechkin beat out Crosby for the 2006 Calder Trophy, but as he took home individual awards year after year, he once said that he would "trade them all for one Stanley Cup." The Penguins ended Ovi's dream in 2016 and 2017 on their way to consecutive titles, and each of Crosby's three Stanley Cups went through Washington in the second round.

But in 2018 the script was flipped. The Capitals beat the Penguins in the second round on their way to the first Stanley Cup in franchise history. Ovechkin had 15 goals and 27 points in 24 games to be named the Conn Smythe Trophy winner.

The 6-foot-3, 239-pound Muscovite wrecking ball then took to the streets for a celebration that was historic in scale and social media exposure.

Ovechkin was handed the Cup in Las Vegas after beating the expansion Vegas Golden Knights, and it stayed with him at a nightclub until 5 a.m. Back in Washington he threw out the first pitch at a Washington Nationals game before doing a keg stand with the Cup and taking it for a swim in a fountain in Georgetown. He later brought it to The Tonight Show and showed it a good time around Moscow, including sitting with it to watch the motherland beat Spain at the 2018 World Cup.

The 2021–22 season saw the Capitals ousted in the first round for the fourth year in a row since winning the Cup, this time by the President's Trophy-winning Florida Panthers, but it was also when the impossible started to feel plausible for Ovechkin.

At 36 Ovechkin scored 50 goals for the ninth time, tying him with Wayne Gretzky and Mike Bossy, and 90 points were his highest total since getting 109 in 2009–10. He now sits third in history with 780 goals and counting, behind only Gordie Howe (801) and Gretzky (894). Gretzky's record, once considered untouchable, is suddenly looking vulnerable.

With a five-year, $47.5 million contract that runs through the 2025–26 season, when he'll be 40, Ovechkin needs 28.5 goals a season to get there. He's averaged almost 46 in his career, and that's counting two pandemic-shortened seasons.

Ovechkin was drawn into a geopolitical storm after Russia invaded Ukraine in February 2022 and he was hesitant to condemn it unequivocally. He didn't do himself any favours by keeping his Instagram profile picture with Vladimir Putin either.

Ovechkin's position as his generation's most unstoppable goal-scorer is secure, and he may retire as the greatest in history, but he missed an open shot at leaving a different kind of legacy.

Won gold at the 2008, 2012 and 2014 World Championship

Won the Hart Trophy three times (2008, 2009, 2013) and the Ted Lindsay Award three times (2008, 2009, 2010)

Won the Art Ross Trophy in 2008

Won the Maurice Richard Trophy nine times (2008, 2009, 2013, 2014, 2015, 2016, 2018, 2019, 2020)

Won the Stanley Cup in 2018 and named Conn Smythe Trophy winner

Tied the NHL record with nine 50-goal seasons in 2021–22

ARTEMI PANARIN

Rangers | Left Wing | 10

When Artemi Panarin was just 3 months old, his parents divorced and he was adopted by his grandparents, Nina and Vladimir Levin. It was just a few years after the Iron Curtain fell and Korkino, their mining town of 40,000 people some 1,000 miles east of Moscow was impoverished.

Short on resources but very resourceful, his grandparents found a way to outfit the scrawny kid for hockey, Vladimir's passion as a young man. His first skates were figure skates and his second were so big he wore shoes inside them. His gloves had no palms so Nina sewed boot leather in, and she fashioned his hockey sweaters out of scrap material.

At 13 Panarin was cut from the top team and considered giving up hockey, but a friend's father got him a spot at a boarding school and hockey program in Podolsk. He was finally given proper hockey equipment and started to grow into his body and potential.

An unheralded player entering the 2011 World Junior Championship in Buffalo, Panarin made a name for himself in the championship game. Russia trailed Canada 3-0 after two periods in front of a heavily partisan crowd, but he scored 2:33 into the third period to spur a comeback and got the gold medal-winner with 4:38 remaining in a 5-3 victory.

Even still, Panarin went undrafted and played seven

seasons in the KHL. He went out on top in his final season of 2014–15 with 62 points in 54 games, and another 20 in 20 playoff games to help SKA St. Petersburg win the Gagarin Cup. He then had five goals and 10 points in 10 games with Russia to earn silver at the 2015 World Championship.

Panarin signed with the Chicago Blackhawks as a free agent in 2015 and in his first NHL training camp he was dubbed "Breadman," after Panera Bread, so he wouldn't be confused with new linemate Artem Anisimov. With Patrick Kane as their third, the line stuck and so did the name.

Panarin scored in his NHL debut against the New York Rangers and had 21 points in his first 19 games. He finished 2015–16 with 30 goals and 77 points, good for ninth in the NHL, to win the Calder Trophy.

After a 31-goal, 74-point season in 2016–17, the Blackhawks traded Panarin to the Columbus Blue Jackets to get Brandon Saad back. Not the Blackhawks' most savvy move, Panarin thrived with his new team, leading the Blue Jackets with 59 assists and 87 points, both franchise records, while Saad had 35 points.

The Blue Jackets made a strong pitch to keep Panarin, but the free agent signed a seven-year, $81.5 million contract with the Rangers in 2019. He made an instant impact again, scoring in his first two games and putting together two 12-game point streaks. He finished with 32 goals, 63 assists and 95 points in just 68 games, all career highs. He led the NHL in even-strength points (71) and was tied for second in assists, second with a plus-36 rating, and tied for third in points. He was also a Hart Trophy and Ted Lindsay Award finalist.

A childhood without much hope made Panarin appreciate his good fortune, and he's been a fun-loving dressing room favorite at every stop. "He's got an unbelievable personality, and the guys completely love him," said linemate Ryan Strome.

It also made him one of the rare Russian athletes willing to criticize the political regime in his homeland. In 2019 Panarin said Vladimir Putin "no longer understands what's right and what's wrong."

In 2021 Panarin spoke in support of jailed opposition leader, Alexi Navalny, and a false accusation of Panarin assaulting a woman a decade earlier came out

of Russia as revenge. He took a leave of absence to deal with the allegations and threats against his family.

Panarin kept his thoughts on Putin and his social media private in 2022. It was a sober reminder during a season in which he set new career highs with 74 assists and 96 points and the Rangers went to the Eastern Conference Final, which they did thanks to Panarin living out every hockey player's fantasy with an overtime winner in Game 7 of round one.

Since his first NHL season Panarin is third in the NHL in assists (382) and fourth in points (569). The players ahead of him are Hart Trophy winners. No one can match his journey or his courage, though.

Won gold at the 2011 World Junior Championship

Won the KHL's Gagarin Cup in 2015

Won the 2016 Calder Trophy

Led the World Championship in assists (13) and points (17) and won bronze in 2017

Hart Trophy and Ted Lindsay Award finalist in 2020

ADAM FOX

Rangers | Defense | 23

Like a lot of young hockey lovers, Adam Fox played for countless hours in his basement, and like a lot of younger siblings, he was put in net. "They would fire the pucks at me and as a little kid it wouldn't bother me," he remembers. "I never wanted to be a goalie; I always wanted to be a forward, but I ended up on defense in real hockey. It turned out to be pretty good."

That's an understatement. The native of Jericho, New York, was already drawing attention by age 3 at IceWorks in Syosset. "I was watching him skate in a long Rangers jersey past his knees — which is really ironic — and right away I was like, 'Who is this kid?

Where is this kid coming from? What's he about?' Just from the way he skated," remembers Mike Bracco, who would coach Fox for years.

His parents, Tammy and Bruce, were diehard Rangers fans and season ticket holders, despite living on Long Island, and their son's bar mitzvah had a hockey theme.

Fox started at forward and always played an age group ahead, but it was on the blue line with the Long Island Gulls that he caught the eye of the U.S. National Team Development Program. He left home at 16 to join the team and ended up breaking the record for assists in a season with 59 in 2015–2016.

The Calgary Flames drafted Fox in the third round, 66th overall, in 2016 but he chose to go to Harvard. "I wasn't really looking for a future in hockey," he says. "I think, first and foremost, the education was the number one reason for wanting to go there."

At Harvard, Fox was a psychology major and led all NCAA defensemen in points-per-game as the Crimson reached the national semifinals in 2016–17. In 2018–19, he had 39 assists in 33 games and was first on the team and second among NCAA defensemen in scoring with 48 points. He was named the Ivy League Player of the Year and was a finalist for the Hobey Baker Award.

Fox had 116 points (21 goals, 95 assists) in 97 games at Harvard and also played for Team USA at two World Junior Championships while he was there, winning gold in 2017 and bronze in 2018.

When it looked like the Flames wouldn't come to terms with Fox, they traded his rights to the Carolina Hurricanes in the 2018 blockbuster alongside Dougie Hamilton for Elias Lindholm and Noah Hanifin. Less than a year later, the Hurricanes faced a similar dilemma and were loaded on defense so they dealt Fox to the Rangers for a second-round and a third-round pick. It's a trade that Carolina might want back.

Fox played his first NHL game in 2019 and had 42 points in 70 games of his rookie season, while skating 18:54 a night. In the pandemic-shortened 2020–2021

season, he upped that to a team-leading 24:42 and was first among NHL defensemen with 42 assists in 55 games and second with 47 points, one point behind the leader. He became the first Ranger to win the Norris Trophy since Brian Leetch in 1996–97 and the second to win it in his sophomore season after Bobby Orr in 1968. He was also the first Jewish player in NHL history to receive a major individual award.

In the offseason, Fox completed his Harvard degree, and then finished third among NHL defensemen in 2021–22 with 63 assists and fourth with 74 points to lead the Rangers back to the playoffs for the first time since 2017. In Game 6 of the first round, he had four assists as the Rangers came back from three games to one to knock out the Pittsburgh Penguins, and then eight points in a seven game win over the Hurricanes. He had 10 points in the Rangers' five elimination games, the most ever for a defenseman in a single postseason. When the Rangers were dismissed by the Tampa Bay Lightning in the Eastern Conference Final, he was leading all NHL defensemen with 18 assists

and 23 points in 23 games.

Fox's parents are back at almost every Rangers home game, while his commute from the Upper West Side apartment he shares with defense partner and former teammate from the USNTDP and Team USA Ryan Lindgren is a little shorter. With a seven-year contract worth $9.5 million a year, the richest ever for a defenseman after his entry-level contract, he could probably afford his own place, even with Manhattan real estate prices, but he needs someone to compete with on his portable putting green. This one lives on the rooftop patio, when New York weather allows, and nobody's firing the ball at anyone else.

Won gold at the 2017 World Junior Championship	
Named Ivy League Player of the Year and a Hobey Baker finalist in 2018–19	
Led all NHL defensemen with 42 assists and won the Norris Trophy in 2020–21	
Selected for the 2022 All-Star Game	

KRIS LETANG

Penguins | Defense | 58

On the morning of January 29, 2014, Kris Letang woke up dizzy and disoriented. Determined to go on the Pittsburgh Penguins' mother-son road trip, he ignored the symptoms and got on the plane.

Team doctor Dharmesh Vyas didn't let Letang play that night in Los Angeles and arranged for an MRI the next day when the Penguins were in Arizona. Letang, at 26, had suffered a stroke. It was the result of an undiagnosed heart defect that's common in babies but usually repairs itself.

"The whole time, he maintained a really strong perspective on what was going on, but also [remained] extremely optimistic that he was going to continue to play," said Vyas.

That perspective was hard earned, because the specter of an athletic career cut short doesn't compare to what Letang had already endured.

In 2003 the Quebec Major Junior Hockey League's Val-d'Or Foreurs drafted Luc Bourdon third overall and Letang 27th. During the 2004–05 season, Bourdon and Letang each had 13 goals and 19 assists in 70 games, and together they won gold medals with Team Canada at the 2006 and 2007 World Juniors.

Bourdon was drafted 10th overall by the Vancouver Canucks in 2005 while the Penguins took Letang 62nd, and they remained close as their NHL careers took off. After winning the Emile Bouchard Trophy as the QMJHL's Defenseman of the Year in 2007, Letang reached the Stanley Cup Final in his first full season with the Penguins. On May 29, 2008, as Pittsburgh was battling Detroit for the Cup, Bourdon died in a motorcycle crash in New Brunswick at the age of 21.

One year later, after the Penguins defeated the Red Wings in a Stanley Cup rematch, Letang got a tattoo dedicated to his grandmother and Bourdon.

"Every time I step on the ice he's in my thoughts," said Letang. "He was a guy that embraced every day of hockey. Every night I think about him before games, making sure I'm ready and all the things he taught me."

With that inspiration, Letang established himself as a young star and the anchor of the Penguins defense — a smooth-skating, puck-moving defenseman who eats minutes and can be deployed in any situation.

Letang was a Norris Trophy finalist after 38 points in 35 games in the lockout-shortened 2012–13 season, but between 2011 and 2015 he missed 102 games due to ailments, including multiple concussions. When Letang has been healthy he's averaged 0.69 points per game, which is third among defensemen with at least 500 games played since he entered the league, and he's third in points with 650.

Back to full strength in 2015–16, Letang averaged almost 27 minutes a game and was third among defensemen with 67 points. In the postseason he averaged just under 29 minutes and had 15 points in 23 games, including the Stanley Cup–winning goal in Game 6 against the San Jose Sharks.

The Penguins repeated as champions in 2017, and despite not playing in the postseason, Letang got his name on the Cup for the third time. He played the minimum 41 regular-season games to be eligible before neck surgery to repair a herniated disc ended his season. During the playoffs he acted as a de facto assistant coach, imparting veteran wisdom and offering inspiration.

Aging like fine wine, Letang played in his sixth All-Star Game in 2020 and in 2021–22, at the age of 34, he set career highs with 58 assists and 68 points, which was tied for sixth among NHL defensemen in scoring, in the last season of his eight-year contract.

After the Penguins were eliminated in overtime of Game 7 in the first round against the New York Rangers, Letang, who averaged 29:51 a game, said he'd like to play another five years. The Penguins also have a vested interest in keeping Sidney Crosby's good friends around. Evgeni Malkin was also a free agent, and the three had played together for 16 seasons, the most by any trio in NHL history. They have three Cups together and they've been the most winning regular season and playoff team in the NHL during their time together, including 16 straight playoff appearances, the longest active streak in North American pro sports.

"There's a bond between them I think is unbreakable," says Penguins goalie Tristan Jarry.

Friendship matters, and while the salary cap is unsentimental, the Penguins found a way to keep all three. They signed their all-time leader among blue-liners in goals, assists and points to a six-year, $36.6 million contract extension.

"Kris epitomizes what it means to be a Pittsburgh Penguin," said general manager Ron Hextall. "The role he plays on our team is irreplaceable."

Won gold at the 2006 and 2007 World Junior Championship

Named the QMJHL's Defenseman of the Year in 2007

Won the Stanley Cup three times (2009, 2016, 2017)

Played in six NHL All-Star Games (2011, 2012, 2016, 2018, 2019, 2020)

IGOR SHESTERKIN

Rangers | Goalie | 31

Igor Shesterkin went 2,020 days between being drafted and playing his first NHL game. In the midst of "King" Henrik Lundqvist's reign in New York, the Rangers had the foresight to select Shesterkin in the fourth round, 118th overall, in 2014 and let him develop in the KHL. It was time well spent.

From 2016–17 through 2018–19, Shesterkin had a 71-12-10 record for SKA St. Petersburg and won a Gagarin Cup. In his final season, he went 24-4-0 with a miniscule 1.11 goals-against average and .953 save percentage.

The native of Moscow signed a contract with the Rangers and came to North America in 2019. He started in the American Hockey League with the Hartford Wolf Pack because the NHL crease was crowded, but with a 17-4-3 record, a 1.90 goals-against average and a .934 save percentage, he forced the Rangers' hand.

Called up in January 2020, Shesterkin won his NHL debut and proceeded to go 10-2-0 with a 2.52 goals-against average and .922 save percentage to essentially dethrone the aging King.

The Rangers retired Lundqvist's number in 2022, ten years after number 30 won his only Vezina Trophy and finished third in Hart Trophy. At season's end, number 31 matched him exactly, taking home his first Vezina and finishing behind Auston Matthews and Connor McDavid as a Hart finalist.

In 2021–22, a season when NHL scoring was at a 30-year high and the average save percentage of .907 was a 15-year low, Shesterkin led the league with a .935 save percentage. His goals-against average of 2.07 was also tops in the NHL and the second lowest in Rangers history, behind Lundqvist's 1.97 in his Vezina year. With a record of 36-13-4 he was three wins behind first place Andrei Vasilevskiy of the Tampa Bay Lightning in ten fewer games played.

A little smaller than Vasilevskiy at 6-foot-1 and 189 pounds, Shesterkin relies on flexibility, agility and a tremendous hockey IQ that lets him read the play and anticipate shots before they happen. "He seems to know what's going to happen before it does," said TNT analyst and former Ranger Eddie Olczyk. "When that happens, you're playing five-card stud with six cards."

Back in the playoffs for the first time since 2017, in Game 1 of the first round, Shesterkin set a Rangers record with 79 saves in a triple overtime loss to the Pittsburgh Penguins. It topped Mike Richter's 1991 mark by 20 shots, and it was the second highest save total in NHL playoff history.

Shesterkin struggled a little after that; he was pulled in Games 3 and 4 as Pittsburgh took a three games to one series lead, and fans in Pittsburgh chanted "Eee-gor" derisively. But coach Gerard Gallant kept the faith and Shesterkin righted the ship. The Rangers won the next three, taking Game 7 in overtime.

In 2014 Lundqvist led the Rangers to the Stanley Cup Final and Shesterkin almost matched that too. In Game 2 of the Eastern Conference Final the Madison Square Garden crowd chanted "Eee-gor's be-tter" as the Rangers opened the series with two wins over the two-time defending champion Lightning. It was a reference to former Vezina and reigning Conn Smythe Trophy winner Vasilevskiy at the other end.

"This is a huge story in Russia right now," said Steve Valiquette, an MSG analyst and goalie who played in the NHL and KHL. "This is like a battle for supremacy. And a lot of people think that Igor can take over the crown."

From Game 5 against the Penguins, over seven games against the Carolina Hurricanes, and through Game 2 of the Eastern Conference Final, Shesterkin was 9-3 with a 2.08 goals-against and a .939 save percentage. He also had three assists, including a game in which he became just the fifth goalie in NHL playoff history with two assists, a highlight reel saucer pass to the far blueline on the tape of Mika Zibanejad. It set a franchise record for goalie points in the postseason and was one behind Martin Brodeur's NHL record set in 2012.

To look at it analytically, since the 2009–10 playoffs there have been 104 times a goalie played at least 500 minutes in a single postseason. Of those, Shesterkin has faced more expected goals and high-danger shots and had to make more high-danger saves than any of them. The Rangers wheel freely and only get away with it because of their goalie.

So the MSG chant was technically accurate, if a little premature as the Lightning came roaring back and took the series in six games. To his credit, Shesterkin called Vasilevskiy "the best goalie in the world right now," even with that series lead.

He wasn't wrong, but the gap is tightening.

Won the KHL's Gagarin Cup in 2017

Led the KHL in goals-against average (1.11) and save percentage (.953) in 2018–19

Led the NHL in goals-against average (2.07) and save percentage (.935) in 2021–22

Nominated for the Hart Trophy in 2021–22

Won the Vezina Trophy in 2021–22

SEBASTIAN AHO

There are two Sebastian Ahos, and not in a metaphysical warrior on the ice, gentleman off the ice kind of way. There are literally two — Sebastian Johannes Aho, a defenseman from Umea, Sweden, on the western side of the Gulf of Bothnia, who has played 61 games for the New York Islanders over three seasons, and Sebastian Antero Aho, a Carolina Hurricanes forward from Rauma, Finland, on the eastern side of the gulf, who led his team in scoring and played in his second All-Star Game in 2021–22. This is about the latter.

The Finnish Aho was chosen by the Hurricanes in the second round, 35th overall, of the 2015 NHL draft as he watched on his laptop in Helsinki. Swedish Aho was eligible but wasn't drafted until 2017.

"We saw this kid and loved him," said then-Hurricanes general manager Ron Francis. "I just wanted to make sure we got the forward. That's the one we wanted."

After being drafted by Carolina, Aho spent another season with Finland's Oulun Karpat, where his father, Harri, played and now works as sports director. "It was my dream to play for Karpat my whole childhood. When I got to play for them, it was huge," said Aho.

Aho had 45 points in 45 games in the Liiga in 2015–16, and over the holidays he played on a line with 2016 draft studs Patrik Laine and Jesse Puljujarvi at the World Juniors. The host Finns beat Russia for gold, and the linemates were the three top scorers in the tournament. Aho's 14 points in seven games were sandwiched between them, just as he was as the center and defensive conscience of the line.

There's a steep learning curve at center in the NHL and Aho started on the wing. He had 49 points in his rookie year, which climbed to 65 in 2017–18. At season's end he shone on the international stage once again with nine goals and 18 points and a plus-15 in eight games at the 2018 World Championship. He was second in tournament scoring behind Patrick Kane and first in points per game at 2.25. Although Finland lost in the quarterfinals he was named the tournament's best forward.

When former Hurricane Rod Brind'Amour took over as head coach in 2018–19 he was initially reluctant to move Aho to center. But the veteran of over 1,600 NHL regular and postseason games knew his young star was ready for the added responsibility.

Aho began the season with a 12-game point streak that included at least one assist in each game, both of which set franchise records and matched Wayne Gretzky (1982–83) and Ken Linseman (1985–86) as the only players to have an assist in the first 12 games to start a season. Aho finished with a team-leading 30

goals and 83 points in 82 games and was the Hurricanes' All-Star Game representative.

A torrid second half earned the Hurricanes a wild-card playoff berth, their first since 2009. The "bunch of jerks," as broadcaster Don Cherry called them in reference to their choreographed victory celebrations, surprised the hockey world by upsetting the defending Stanley Cup champion Washington Capitals in seven games and then sweeping the Islanders. Aho led the team again in the postseason with 12 points in 15 games.

That inspired the first offer sheet the NHL had seen in six years, tendered by the Montreal Canadiens to the restricted free agent. The Hurricanes quickly matched it to keep their most talented player and future leader, and then made a revenge offer to compatriot and Canadien Jesperi Kotkaniemi in 2021 with a cheeky $20 signing bonus to match Aho's sweater number, which Montreal didn't match.

On March 31, 2022, the two Sebastian Ahos scored 34 seconds apart — in two different games and cities — but only the Finnish one went to the playoffs, after leading his team in goals (37), assists (44) and points (81) and playing in his second All-Star Game.

The Hurricanes beat the Boston Bruins in seven games before losing in seven to the New York Rangers. Aho tied for the team lead in playoff scoring with 11 points in 14 games, passing both Brind'Amour and former captain Eric Staal along the way to become the franchise's all-time leader in postseason scoring with 46 points in 48 games.

It wasn't much consolation for Aho, who spoke of the "anger" and "disappointment" he felt after being eliminated, which would fuel his offseason workouts. Still just 25, he has room to grow and another level to get to before his name is spoken among the NHL's truly elite.

Won gold at the 2016 World Junior Championship
Named best forward at the 2018 World Championship
Set franchise records in 2018–19 with a 12-game point streak that included at least one assist in each game to start the season
Played in two NHL All-Star Games (2019, 2022)
Hurricanes' franchise leader in career playoff points (46)

EVGENI MALKIN

Penguins | Center | 71

A t the 2017 All-Star weekend, the NHL named its top 100 players from its first 100 years. There were six active players on the list. Evgeni Malkin wasn't one of them.

These types of lists are hotly debated, but Geno was a glaring omission. There are few NHL players more decorated than Malkin, but one happens to be on his team, and that might explain the snub.

Malkin was born in Magnitogorsk, Russia, an iron and steel town on the Ural River. The resources gave the Metallurg hockey team its name, and he joined its system when he was 5 years old. At 17 Malkin was signed to Metallurg's senior team for the 2003–04 season. At the end of the year he was one of the greatest consolation prizes in NHL draft history, going

second overall to the Pittsburgh Penguins, after the Washington Capitals took Alex Ovechkin.

Malkin played two more years in Magnitogorsk and had signed the richest contract in the Russian Super League, but he longed to be in the U.S. He left the team during training camp in Helsinki and hid out until he could get his American visa. "This is pure sports terrorism," said Metallurg general manager Gennady Velichkin, who tried to sue the Penguins.

Sidney Crosby had already arrived in Pittsburgh as the top pick in 2005, and it soon became apparent that the Penguins had the 21st century version of Mario Lemieux and Jaromir Jagr.

Malkin made his Penguins debut in 2006–07 and didn't disappoint. He set a modern-day record by scoring in each of his first six games. The only other player to do that was Joe Malone of the Montreal Canadiens in 1917–18. Malkin finished the year with 33 goals, 85 points and the Calder Trophy.

The Penguins lost the 2008 Stanley Cup Final to the Detroit Red Wings, after Malkin had 106 regular-season points. A year later he led the league in scoring with 113 points, and the Penguins beat Detroit in a rematch to win the Cup. With 14 goals and 36 points in 24 games, Malkin became the second-youngest player in history to win the Conn Smythe Trophy.

Over his first four seasons Malkin was one of only three players to average more than a point a game each year, Crosby and Ovechkin being the other two. In 2011 he was averaging just under a point a game when he tore his ACL and MCL, ending his season.

Malkin returned in 2011–12 with a chip on his shoulder and the team on his back. With Crosby suffering from post-concussion syndrome, Malkin had a career-high 50 goals and 109 points to win his second Art Ross. He also won the Hart Trophy and the Ted Lindsay Award.

At 6-foot-3 and 195 pounds, Malkin can do it with power and finesse, a rare combination that's reminiscent of Lemieux. "In sheer skill level Geno probably has to be rated higher [than Crosby]," said former Pittsburgh coach Dan Bylsma. "There's magic there, a little bit different than what Sid has."

Together Malkin and Crosby won their second Stanley Cup in 2016 and then went past Lemieux and Jagr with a third in 2017. Malkin led all scorers with 28 points in the playoffs that season.

While the Penguins celebrated, general manager Jim Rutherford mused about the 100 Greatest Players list of a few months earlier. "Maybe we can revote and see if Malkin is in the top 100 now."

Malkin further built his case with a 98-point season in 2017–18. A rib injury slowed him in 2018–19 and limited him to 68 games, but he still had 72 points and broke the 1,000 career points barrier.

After 42 points in 41 games in 2021–22 because of knee surgery that cost him the first three months of the season, Malkin is now fourth in goals (444) and points (1,146) since he made his NHL debut, and his 1.17 points per game trail only Connor McDavid and Crosby.

The season concluded with a 16th consecutive trip to the postseason but a fourth straight first round exit and the end of Malkin's eight-year contract. After dangling the idea of free agency, he signed a four-year, $24.4 million extension.

The 36-year-old has dealt with a series of injuries over the last several seasons that have cost him significant time, but Malkin still thinks he has elite hockey in him: "I believe in my body. I believe in myself."

The 100 Greatest NHL Players panel may have disagreed, but whenever it happens, the Hall of Fame Selection Committee will surely be on Malkin's side.

Won the Calder Trophy in 2007	
Won the Stanley Cup three times (2009, 2016, 2017)	
Won the Conn Smythe Trophy in 2009	
Won the Art Ross Trophy twice (2009, 2012)	
Won the Hart Trophy and Ted Lindsay Award in 2012	

MIKA ZIBANEJAD

Rangers | Center | 93

T he Ottawa Senators drafted Mika Zibanejad sixth overall in 2011, though that didn't
impress his father much.

"Yesterday we enjoyed it, but that was yesterday and
today we go back to business and take care of the plan
for the future," said his dad, Mehrdad, an IT engineer
with the Swedish government.

Mehrdad lived through the Iranian revolution in
1979 and was jailed for writing against it. He was
then forced to fight in the Iran/Iraq war as part of his
mandatory military service, so he has a more nuanced
perspective than most hockey parents.

After Mehrdad had fulfilled his military obligation
he immigrated to Sweden in 1983, where he met his
Finnish-born wife, Ritva. Mika was born in 1993 in
Huddinge, just south of Stockholm.

Inspired by his older half-brother, Monir Kalgoum,
Mika took up the game at seven but didn't start to
stand out "until 15 or 16," by his own estimation.
He played for Djurgarden's under-18 and under-20
teams before making his debut in the Swedish Hockey
League in 2010 at 17. The following season, at just
18 years and 172 days old, he played in his first NHL
game, becoming the youngest Swede ever to play in an
NHL game and the youngest player in Sens history.

After nine games the Senators sent Zibanejad back
to Djurgarden, and at the 2012 World Junior Championship he scored the golden goal in overtime to give
Sweden a 1–0 victory over Russia and the country's
first World Junior title in 31 years.

NHL players were locked out to start the 2012–13
season, so Zibanejad started the year with the

American Hockey League's Binghamton Senators. Called up when the season began, he scored his first NHL goal on January 30, 2013.

In 2015–16 Zibanejad posted career highs in games played (81), goals (21), assists (30) and points (51). Then in the summer of 2016, just days after he'd moved into a new home, the Senators shocked Zibanejad by trading him to the New York Rangers for Derek Brassard.

Zibanejad embraced big city life and the relative anonymity that Manhattan affords a hockey player. The move was also popular with his friends back home, who were more familiar with the Original Six franchise that had Swedish legend Henrik Lundqvist minding the net.

Zibanejad had 15 points in his first 19 games with the Rangers before breaking his left fibula in November 2016, costing him 25 games. The following November he suffered a concussion that put him out of the lineup for nine games, so it was satisfying to play all 82 games in 2018–19.

The 6-foot-2, 200-pound Zibanejad reached the 30-goal plateau for the first time, becoming the first Rangers center to get there since Eric Lindros in 2001–02. He had 74 points, 23 more than his previous career best, and he also set career highs in assists, average ice time, shots on goal, faceoff wins and takeaways.

Zibanejad, who was named an alternate captain prior to the season, led the team in goals, assists, points, power-play goals, power-play assists, power-play points, shots on goal, takeaways and faceoff wins. He also had a hand in 10 consecutive goals scored by the Rangers, from January 19 to February 4, the first player in franchise history to do so.

Zibanejad was just getting started though. He set a new career high with 41 goals and 75 points in just 57 games in 2019–20, including a five-goal game against the Washington Capitals. After getting 50 points in 56

games the following season, he had 52 assists and 81 points in 81 games in 2021–22.

With his flowing locks and facial hair, Zibanejad took his swashbuckler act into the postseason, scoring big goals and having fun doing it. He had seven points in the last two games against the Pittsburgh Penguins as the Rangers erased a three games to one series deficit, including the tying goal with 5:45 left in the Rangers season in Game 7, and a four-game goal streak in another seven game win over the Carolina Hurricanes.

When the Rangers were eliminated by the Tampa Bay Lightning in the Eastern Conference Final, Zibanejad was tied for the team lead in goals with 10 and first with 24 points in 20 games. That put him third in the NHL behind Connor McDavid and Leon Draisaitl, who had two of the highest-scoring playoffs in NHL history at that point.

With a new eight-year, $68 million contract, postseason exposure and success after four years on the outside looking in, and a side hustle as a DJ and music producer, Zibanejad is a bona fide star on Broadway.

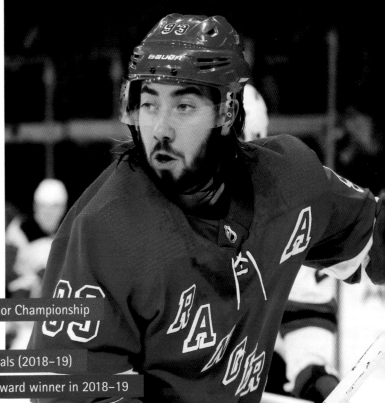

Scored the overtime goal to win gold at the 2012 World Junior Championship

Won gold at the 2018 World Championship

Became the first Ranger with a point on 10 straight team goals (2018–19)

Voted Rangers MVP and the Steven McDonald Extra Effort Award winner in 2018–19

JOHN CARLSON

Capitals | Defense | 74

teams' top units and top lines, in my eyes, he's the best defenseman in the league," says teammate T.J. Oshie.

Born in Natick, Massachusetts, and raised in Colonia, New Jersey, Carlson idolized the New Jersey Devils' Scott Stevens while playing for the New Jersey Rockets. He graduated from there to the Indiana Ice of the United States Hockey League at the age of 17 and was drafted 27th overall by the Capitals in 2008.

Carlson then chose to play for the Ontario Hockey League's London Knights and in his one season in London he was named the Knights' MVP. He had 76 points (16 goals, 60 assists) in 59 games and 22 more (seven goals, 15 assists) in 14 postseason games.

After the Knights were eliminated in the third round, Carlson joined the Hershey Bears for the American Hockey League playoffs and helped them win the 2009 Calder Cup.

Carlson had a brief NHL cameo early in 2009–10 before being sent back down to the minors and joining Team USA for the 2010 World Juniors. He scored the golden goal in overtime against Canada in the championship game, earning the U.S. its first gold since 2004. It was his second goal of the game and he was named to the all-tournament team.

Carlson was back with the Capitals late in the season, but after they were eliminated by the Montreal Canadiens he joined Hershey for the AHL playoffs and added to his clutch credentials by scoring the goal that won the Bears their second straight Calder Cup.

In the NHL, by 2010–11, Carlson was named to the All-Rookie Team and came fifth in Calder Trophy voting after earning 37 points. Since then he's second among all NHL defensemen in assists (456) and third in points (587).

After finishing the 2017–18 season with career highs in goals (15), assists (53) and points (68), Carlson took it to another level in the playoffs, again leading all defensemen in points with 20 (five goals, 15 assists) and a plus-11 rating in 24 games as the Capitals

L eading the NHL in any offensive category generally leads to trophy recognition, but not if you're John Carlson, and that's okay with him.

After being first among defensemen in scoring in 2017–18, Carlson finished a distant fifth in Norris Trophy voting. He was five points ahead of winner Victor Hedman but 91 first-place votes adrift.

Granted, there's far more to defense than points, but Carlson is as complete as they come. "Everyone talks about the points he has, which are pretty amazing and pretty special, but with his play all around, playing PK, playing big minutes defensively, playing against other

won the franchise's first Stanley Cup after years of disappointment.

The 6-foot-3, 218-pound defenseman signed an eight-year, $64 million contract just before he hit the free agent market in 2018, but far from being complacent with the money, Carlson upped his career highs in assists (57) as well as points (70), while averaging a new career high in ice time at 25:04. He also went to his first All-Star Game and won the hardest shot competition with a 102.8-mile-per-hour slap shot, topping Alex Ovechkin's 101.3-mile-per-hour winner from the year prior for dressing room bragging rights.

In 2019–20 Carlson was on his way to becoming the first defensemen with 90 points since Ray Bourque in 1993–94, and just the ninth to ever do it, but the pandemic had other ideas. When the NHL ended the regular season early, he was first on the Capitals in scoring, eight points ahead of Ovechkin, and he led all NHL defensemen in assists (60) and points (75) again, 11 assists and 10 points ahead of second place Roman Josi.

He finished second in Norris voting to Josi, which was Carlson's highest showing, but as he said before, it's the Stanley Cup that matters: "At the end of the day, I got what I wanted."

In 2021–22 Carlson set a career high with 17 goals and finished fifth among defensemen with 71 points, but it was the fourth straight year the Capitals lost in the first round of the playoffs.

Even that can be put in perspective for Carlson. When he had his day with the Cup, he took it to the Children's National Hospital in Washington, and he and his wife, Gina, held a fundraiser to fight childhood brain cancer.

"I've been around a little bit now to where some kids are out of the hospital, and they'll come up to me, 'Hey, remember you brought (the Cup)?'" said Carlson. "It's real heartwarming to see or to hear those stories of warriors."

Never mind the individual awards, some things are even bigger than the Cup.

ZACH WERENSKI

Blue Jackets | Defense | 8

Zach Werenski was determined to enter college a year early so he completed his entire senior year of high school in one summer. The native of Grosse Pointe, Michigan, had already started at the University of Michigan when he returned home to write one last exam.

At 17 Werenski was the youngest player in the NCAA, yet he was already 6-foot-2 and over 200 pounds as a freshman. He led the Wolverines defense in scoring and the conference in goals among defensemen, and he was named to the All-Big Ten first team as well as the Big Ten All-Freshman team. "He looked like a senior, just the way he was built," said Oiler Zach Hyman of his former Michigan teammate.

It wasn't just his size that impressed. The Werenskis were devoted Detroit Red Wings fans, and Zach grew up admiring Nicklas Lidstrom, particularly his calmness with the puck, which he brought to his own game.

The Blue Jackets liked his combination of size and serenity and drafted Werenski eighth overall in 2015.

Returning to Michigan for his sophomore season, he ranked second in scoring among all NCAA defenders and captained the bronze medal–winning Team USA at the 2016 World Juniors. He led all defensemen with nine points and all skaters with a plus-10 rating en route to being named the best defenseman.

Werenski got his first taste of professional hockey toward the end of the 2015–16 American Hockey League season. He joined the Lake Erie Monsters for the last seven games of the regular season and the playoffs. Werenski had nine assists and 14 points in 17 postseason games as the Monsters won the Calder

Cup. He ranked second among AHL defensemen in playoff scoring, with the most assists and points by an 18-year-old in AHL playoff history.

All that was left to conquer was the NHL, and in 2016–17 the rookie had 47 points in 78 games, with a plus-17 rating and only 14 penalty minutes.

The second-youngest defenseman in the NHL, Werenski was the top scorer among rookie blue-liners, was seventh in overall rookie scoring and had the sixth-most points by a rookie teenage defenseman in NHL history. He set a Blue Jackets record for points by a rookie, which was also the second-most points by a defenseman in franchise history. Werenski averaged almost 21 minutes per game and had the best possession rating of all Blue Jackets defensemen.

The 2016–17 season ended a little more painfully, however. In the third game of the playoffs against the Pittsburgh Penguins, a Phil Kessel shot rode up his stick and hit Werenski in the face, leading to a right eye that was 50 shades of black and swollen shut. After trying to play with a full visor, Werenski was taken out of the game and declared finished for the season. "Balls as big as the building," is how then-Blue Jackets coach John Tortorella described Werenski's effort to return to the game.

Werenski was a finalist for the Calder Trophy, so his first year isn't remembered just for the size of his black eye or anything else on his anatomy.

Werenski led all NHL defensemen with 20 goals in the shortened 2019–20 season, and after losing much of the 2020–21 season to a sports hernia, he had career-highs with 37 assists and 48 points in 68 games played in 2021–22. The season ended with another broken nose, after suffering head injuries earlier in the season.

"I'm excited to stop getting hit in the head. I've got too many of those lately," joked Werenski at the end of the season. "I've got to do something this summer to make the hockey gods like me again."

Living up to the six-year, $57.5 million contract he signed before the season, six days after their other star defenseman Seth Jones was traded to the Chicago Blackhawks, Werenski was tied for sixth in the NHL in average ice time with Norris Trophy winner Cale Makar at 25:40 a game, and named an alternate captain.

"He's really a hell of a player, but now he's the lead dog. And you see how he's handling it," said Blue Jackets general manager Jarmo Kekalainen.

"When he told me that he felt like he was always in Jonesy's shadow, I told him: 'You were never there for me.'"

And he's no longer a child prodigy. At 24 Werenski had played almost as many NHL games as the other Blue Jackets defensemen combined. He's now a seasoned defenseman and team leader, and he has the scars to prove it.

Won bronze at the 2016 World Junior Championship and named best defenseman

Named a First Team All-American and Big Ten Defensive Player of the Year in 2016

Voted a finalist for the Calder Trophy in 2017

Set the Blue Jackets record for points by a rookie

Led all NHL defensemen in goals in 2019–20 (20)

Played in two NHL All-Star Games (2018 and 2022)

FREDERIK ANDERSEN

Hurricanes | Goalie | 31

E rnst Andersen was a championship-winning goalie with his hometown Herning Blue Fox in Denmark's top flight, but even as his son Frederik emerged as a star between the pipes he didn't see the NHL in his future.

There wasn't much precedent to go on. Only nine Danes had been drafted before Frans Nielsen, another Herning native, became the first to play in the NHL in 2007. That an Andersen would join him in the world's top league shouldn't have come as much of a surprise, however. The Andersen family is Danish hockey royalty. Ernst played professionally for 20 years before becoming the national junior team's goalie coach, and his wife, Charlotte, also played, as did a handful of their brothers and cousins.

All three of their children followed in their footsteps; Sebastian played defense in Denmark, Amalie played the same position in a women's league in Sweden and "Freddie" has become a star in North America.

With stiff competition in Herning, Andersen went to the Frederikshavn White Hawks in 2009 and had a .932 save percentage in 30 games. Then in 2011–12 he crossed the Kattegat to play for legendary Frolunda in the Swedish Hockey League, where he had a 1.62 goals-against average and .943 save percentage, both of which led the league, and he broke Henrik Lundqvist's franchise record with eight shutouts.

After being passed over in two NHL drafts, Andersen was taken in the last round in 2010 by the Carolina Hurricanes. He never signed a contract, however, so in 2012 the Anaheim Ducks chose Andersen in the third round, 87th overall. On October 20, 2013, he became the first Danish goalie in NHL history.

In 2014–15 Andersen made another mark on the record books as the fastest goalie in NHL history to reach the 26-win mark (26-5-0), and he tied the record for the fastest to 50 career wins (50-13-5), originally set by Bill Durnan of the Montreal Canadiens in 1944.

The following season Andersen had a 22-9-7 record and shared the William M. Jennings Trophy with partner John Gibson for allowing the fewest goals in the league.

Gibson was the starter of the strongest duo in the league, so the Ducks traded Andersen to the Toronto Maple Leafs in 2016 for a first- and second-round pick.

Andersen set a Maple Leafs record for wins in a season in 2017–18 with 38, good for fourth in the league, and after being eliminated by the Boston Bruins, the great Dane put on a show at the arena where he watched his dad and got his start, an arena full of Herning Blue Fox banners and trophies. Denmark fell short of the medals at the 2018 World Championship, but Andersen was named the tournament's best goaltender.

In 2018–19 Andersen tied for third in the NHL with 36 wins but a second straight loss to the Bruins in the playoffs ended a season with great promise, despite Andersen's .922 playoff save percentage. And for the first time, he said no to his country.

The 2020–21 would be his last in Toronto. Over five seasons with the Leafs, Andersen was third in the NHL in games played (268), fourth in wins (149), and second in both shots faced (8,466) and saved (7,740). Those numbers would be even higher if he hadn't suffered a knee injury that limited him to only 24 games, many played through pain.

Jack Campbell took over in the Leafs' crease while Andersen was sidelined, and at the end of the season the unrestricted free agent signed where it all could have begun, in Carolina. It was better late than never, and a heck of a first impression. He was the third goalie in NHL history to win each of his first eight games with a team, and he started 11 of the Hurricanes' first 12 games, winning nine, including one against his former team.

"He's calm and collected and does his job, and he's done a fantastic job," said Ian Cole of his new teammate. "I don't see much more than a smile. Maybe when we beat Toronto. He was pretty happy."

Andersen started 51 games for the Hurricanes in 2021–22, with a record of 35-14-3 and four shutouts. His 2.17 goals-against average was second in the NHL and his .922 save percentage was tied for third, which had him firmly in the Vezina Trophy conversation until an MCL tear in April ended his season early.

The Hurricanes came within one win of the Eastern Conference Final, a disappointment for the team with the second-best record in the NHL and their number one goalie watching in frustration from the press box.

Named to the NHL All-Rookie Team in 2013–14

Shared the William M. Jennings Trophy with John Gibson in 2016

Finished first in the NHL in saves in 2017–18 with 2,029

Named Best Goaltender at the 2018 World Championship

Played in two NHL All-Star Games (2020, 2022)

MATHEW BARZAL

Islanders | Center | 13

Mathew Barzal's first NHL game wasn't exactly the stuff of childhood dreams. Chosen 16th overall in the 2015 NHL Entry Draft by the New York Islanders after they traded up to get him, he was in the lineup on opening night of the 2016–17 season. His box score included three penalties, two in the first 5:06 of the game, four lost faceoffs of six taken, and no shots on net.

"I'd played exhibition games and I'd been through training camp, but there's nothing like playing in a regular-season NHL game," understated Barzal.

Barzal was a healthy scratch for the next five games and then played once more before being sent back to the Seattle Thunderbirds of the Western Hockey League, who had drafted the Coquitlam, British Columbia native and product of the Burnaby Winter Club first in the 2012 bantam draft.

Instead of sulking, Barzal went on to become the WHL's Western Conference Player of the Year after finishing with 10 goals and 79 points in only 41 games. He followed that up by leading Seattle to its first WHL championship and being named the 2017 playoff MVP, with 25 points in 16 games. As an alternate captain for Team Canada, Barzal also had eight points in seven games at the 2017 World Juniors and won silver.

"If you let that stuff hold you back — or if you develop a bitterness toward people — it just takes away from your game, and you have to make the best of it," reasoned Barzal.

And what a difference a year makes. Barzal stuck with the Islanders the following season and led the team with 85 points, becoming the first rookie in franchise history to have five assists in one game in the process. His 63 assists tied a franchise record and was the third-highest total by a rookie in NHL history, and he was also just the fourth rookie in the salary cap era to average more than a point a game while playing more than half the season, joining Alex Ovechkin, Evgeni Malkin, Connor McDavid, and his idol, Sidney Crosby. It made the Calder Trophy voting nearly unanimous — Barzal received 160 of 164 first-place votes.

Barzal's numbers were down in 2018–19, to 18 goals and 62 points, but he was the driving force behind one of the more satisfying moments of a resurgent season for the Islanders under new coach Barry Trotz.

Facing their former captain John Tavares for the first time after he chose his hometown Toronto Maple Leafs in free agency, Barzal had a natural hat trick in less than eight minutes on the way to a 4–0 victory. He was the first Islander with a hat trick against Toronto since Mike Bossy in 1986.

The passionate Islanders fans took great delight in this, and enjoyed a measure of revenge by finishing three points ahead of Toronto and reaching the second round of the playoffs while the Maple Leafs were out in the first.

If the postseason is the measure of success, the Islanders have a decided advantage. While the Maple Leafs continue to lose in the opening round, the Islanders made it to the Stanley Cup semi-final in 2020 and 2021, losing to the eventual champion Tampa Bay Lightning each time, the second in seven games.

In 2021–22 Barzal had 15 goals and 44 assists for 59 points in 73 games after missing time due to an injury for the first time in his career. He was tops on the team in assists and tied Brock Nelson for the team lead in points in the defense-first system of Trotz, who was fired after the Islanders missed the playoffs.

For the first time since Barzal's rookie season, he was free to play for Canada at the World Championship. It was another exercise in getting excruciatingly close. He had eight points in nine games, including the tying goal with less than two minutes left in the quarter-final

against Sweden and an assist on the overtime winner. He also had three assists in another furious comeback in the gold medal match, but Canada lost in overtime to the host Finns.

Still just 25 years-old, Barzal is hitting his stride and prime. "I think he's got two or three more layers that he can take his game to," said one NHL scout of Barzal, who has played in two All-Star Games and won the fastest skater competition in 2020 by upsetting three-time defending champion Connor McDavid.

"He can skate with the puck, wheel and deal, make his teammates better, and he's got a great shot," according to retired NHL player Scott Hartnell. "There's nothing, I don't think, that he can't do."

Won gold at the 2014 Hlinka Gretzky Cup	
Named WHL playoff MVP in 2017	
Won the Calder Trophy in 2018	
Played in two NHL All-Star Games (2019, 2020), winning fastest skater in 2020	
Won silver at the 2022 World Championship	

SEAN COURTURIER

Flyers | Center | 14

venue Sean Couturier leads to the K.C. Irving Centre, home of the Quebec Major Junior Hockey League's Acadie-Bathurst Titan in Bathurst, New Brunswick. That's not who Couturier played for, nor is it where he came into the world.

Couturier was born in Arizona while his father, Sylvain, was playing for the Phoenix Roadrunners of the International Hockey League. Sylvain, a native of Quebec who got into 33 games with the Los Angeles Kings, moved the family to Bathurst in 2002 to join the Titan coaching staff. One of his players was Patrice Bergeron, who Sean must have watched closely.

After dominating in midget in New Brunswick but failing to make the AAA league in Quebec, Couturier found his way to Saskatchewan to play for the storied Notre Dame Hounds, where he had 56 points in 40 games. He then went back to Quebec when the Drummondville Voltigeurs drafted him second overall in the 2008 QMJHL draft.

As a rookie Couturier helped the Voltigeurs win the 2009 league title, and in 2009–10 the 6-foot-3 center was plus-62 and won the Jean Beliveau Trophy as the QMJHL's leading scorer with 41 goals and 55 assists for 96 points.

In 2010–11, Couturier won the Michael Bossy Trophy as the league's top prospect and the Michel Briere Trophy for league MVP after another 96-point season. He was also the youngest player on Canada's entry at the 2011 World Junior Championship and added a silver medal to his trophy case.

What also set Couturier apart was his focus on his own end. "That's where all my offence starts — getting the puck out and going on attack. You want to be that guy at the end of the game that you can count on defensively to shut down and not get scored on," he said in 2010. "You always want to be in those key moments."

The Philadelphia Flyers chose Couturier 8th overall in 2011, after some thought he might go first, and he went straight to the NHL, making a strong impression as a defensive center and earning votes for both the Calder and Selke Trophies. He also became the second youngest player in NHL history to record a postseason hat trick, scoring three against the cross-state rival Pittsburgh Penguins in the first round of the 2012 playoffs.

After a bit of time in the American Hockey League in 2012–13, Couturier was a steady NHL presence with strong underlying stats, but he didn't light it up offensively like he did in junior until 2017–18. Elevated to the top line, he smashed his career highs with 31 goals, 45 assists and 76 points in 82 games, finishing second in Selke Trophy voting.

Couturier also came up big against the Penguins in the playoffs once again, with five goals and four assists in five games, including three goals and two assists in a Game 6 loss that eliminated the Flyers.

As he did in junior, Couturier replicated his high in consecutive seasons with 76 points (33 goals, 43 assists) again in 2018–19.

In the shortened 2019–20, Couturier had 59 points (22 goals, 37 assists) in 69 games, was plus-21, and had an NHL-best faceoff winning percentage of 59.6. He won the Selke Trophy, edging out Bergeron.

The 2020–21 season was challenging at the best of times, and Couturier was playing though a separated rib and a hip flexor problem. He still had 41 points in 45 games, the same point-per-game average (0.91) as he did from 2017–18 through 2019–20, while improving on his five-on-five shots created and attempted.

Despite pandemic and salary cap uncertainty, the Flyers signed Couturier to an eight-year, $62 million contract extension in August 2021 that runs through 2029–2030. He only played 29 games after suffering a back injury in December that ended his season, but even with 142 total games missed since he entered the league, he's ninth in both goals (180) and assists (280) and eighth in points (460) among his draft class, and sits fifth in plus-minus (+82) at the end of the 2021–22 season.

When the Flyers traded captain Claude Giroux before the 2022 trade deadline, it signaled a change of regime, with the 29-year-old Couturier — the longest-serving Flyer, an alternate captain and a three-time winner of the Bobby Clarke Trophy for team MVP — as heir apparent.

After two seasons out of the playoffs, the Flyers' road to respectability will run through Couturier.

Won the 2009–10 Jean Beliveau Trophy as QMJHL leading scorer

Won the Michel Briere Trophy as QMJHL MVP and Michael Bossy Trophy as top prospect in 2010–11

Won silver at the 2011 World Junior Championship

Won gold at the 2015 World Championship

Won silver at the 2017 and 2019 World Championships

Won the 2020 Selke Trophy

CHRIS KREIDER

Just north of Boston, Boxford, Massachusetts, is a quaint little New England town known for its Apple Festival and as the homestead of hockey legend Ray Bourque when he was playing for the Bruins.

It's also quickly becoming famous for the place Chris Kreider grew up. "It's incredible. All my friends and family know he came through our program. So I feel like a celebrity just knowing that they know I know him," according to Andrew Jackson, Kreider's assistant coach at Masconomet Regional High School.

Kreider started out on the junior varsity squad, but before his sophomore year, he grew six inches and both he and the varsity team surged. He also shone in soccer, lacrosse and the classroom, while dreaming

of becoming a professional baseball player. By then he'd outgrown Masconomet and went down the road to attend the prestigious Phillips Academy Andover, where he was a member of the Russian and architecture clubs and took yoga as an elective.

"He was not just a hockey kid. He was a member of the community in so many different ways. He's one of those very special kids. He really is," remembers Andover hockey coach Dean Boylan. "He was certainly an outstanding talent. We knew that when he arrived, but I would certainly be lying if I told you I expected him to be a number one draft pick in the NHL."

First round at least. After the New York Rangers drafted Kreider 19th overall in 2009 he went to Boston College, where he won the 2010 NCAA title in his rookie season. He also had six goals in seven games to help Team USA win gold at the 2010 World Junior Championship, and the teen represented his country at the 2010 World Championship.

In 2011–12 Kreider had 23 goals and 45 points in 44 games and won his second NCAA championship. He signed his first pro contract with the Rangers immediately afterward and made his NHL debut days later in Game 3 of the first round of the playoffs against the Ottawa Senators.

Kreider's first NHL goal was the winner in Game 6, and he also scored the winning goal in Game 1 of the second round against the Washington Capitals. He finished with five goals in 18 playoff games in 2012 to set an NHL record for most postseason goals by a player who hadn't appeared in a regular season game.

A 6-foot-3, 223-pound power forward with speed, Kreider led the forwards with eight points in round two of the 2014 playoffs to help the Rangers reach their first Stanley Cup Final in 20 years. He also took out all-world goalie Carey Price of the Montreal Canadiens in the process, knocking him out in Game 1 with a skates-first slide.

It's where Kreider's reputation as a crease-crasher began, but it's also where he makes his money. He's a master of tips and deflections, with an assist from his baseball training, and he fights for position to bang in rebounds. The goal mouth and the "home plate" area, bounded by the crease and the two faceoff dots, are his domain, and it takes brawn and nifty hands to score from in close like that. Growing up he was known for his speed and dangles with the puck, but the evolution began at Boston College to maximize his assets and help him reach the NHL.

In 2014–15, Kreider was the only NHL player with at least 20 goals, 40 points, a plus-20 rating and 80 penalty minutes. He scored a career-high 28 goals in 2016–17, matched that in 2018–19, and was named to the NHL All-Star Game for the first time in 2020 with 24 goals in the pandemic-shorted 2019–20 season. But he blew those totals away in 2021–22.

Kreider was first in the NHL with 26 power-play goals and hit the magical 50-goal plateau, joining Jaromir Jagr, Adam Graves and Vic

Won gold at the 2010 World Junior Championship	
NCAA champion in 2010 and 2012	
Won bronze at the 2018 World Championship	
Played in two NHL All-Star Games (2020, 2022)	
Led the NHL with 26 powerplay goals in 2021–22	

Hadfield as the only Rangers to get there. He finished with 52 for third in the NHL, sandwiched between Leon Draisaitl and Alex Ovechkin.

And after scoring 10 goals in 20 games in the Rangers' run to the 2022 Eastern Conference Final, including two in Game 7 of the second round to eliminate the Carolina Hurricanes, Kreider is tied with Rod Gilbert atop the franchise's all-time playoff goals list with 34.

Garnet Hathaway, a friend from Phillips Academy and Capitals winger, say it's Kreider's relentless drive that got them both to the NHL. "I consider myself lucky to have been around him to get that competitive push. If you surround yourself with smart, hard-working people who are friendly, that's the best you can do."

DOUGIE HAMILTON

Devils | Defense | 7

The basement of the Hamilton home in St. Catharines, Ontario, is a repository for the accumulated accomplishments of a supremely athletic family. Asked which of the many awards and shiny objects is her favourite, Lynn says the World Junior Championship bronze medals won by her sons, Freddie and Dougie, in 2012 because they were teammates.

Lynn has plenty of her own after representing Canada in basketball at the 1984 Summer Olympics in Los Angeles, where she also met her future husband, Doug, who won a bronze in quad rowing. The point guard earned herself a bronze two years later at the 1986 World Championship.

Freddie was born in Toronto in 1992, and after being drafted in the fifth round by the San Jose Sharks, he played 75 NHL games for four teams. He's now retired and pursuing an MBA at Yale University.

Born 17 months later, Dougie showed equal promise in the classroom and on the ice. Playing for the Niagara IceDogs, where his brother was a teammate, he won the Bobby Smith Trophy as the OHL's Scholastic Player of the Year and the CHL Scholastic Player of the Year Award for the 2010–11 season. He also had 58 points in 67 games and a team-high plus-35.

Picked ninth overall by the Boston Bruins in the 2011 draft, Hamilton was 6-foot-4 and still growing.

Sent back to Niagara for the 2011–12 season, he led all OHL defensemen with 55 assists and 72 points in 50 games and won the Max Kaminsky Trophy as the OHL's Most Outstanding Defenseman and the CHL's Defenseman of the Year.

Hamilton played three seasons in Boston and seemed poised to take over for Zdeno Chara as the alpha defenseman, but the Bruins traded him to the Calgary Flames for two high draft picks in 2015 when his entry level contract expired.

In 2016–17 Hamilton set career highs with 37 assists and 50 points, and the following season, he tied for the NHL lead among defensemen with 17 goals and finished with 44 points. He also convinced management to acquire Freddie, who played 38 games with the Flames over three seasons.

Calgary only made the playoffs once in Dougie's three seasons in Calgary, and a rumored rift developed among teammates. Hockey is not always known as the most enlightened sport, and some players were reportedly upset that Hamilton would choose to go to museums instead of socializing with his fellow Flames.

Traded to the Carolina Hurricanes in a blockbuster five-player deal in 2018, Hamilton responded upon his return to Alberta. "I don't know if I was hurt. It's just a thing that's out there with, I guess, the museums. I've gotten some free passes to some museums in Raleigh now, so, yeah. It is what it is. It's not true, so I just try to laugh at it and believe in myself and who I am as a person."

Hamilton had 18 goals in 2018–19, second among NHL defensemen. In three seasons in Carolina, he had 121 points, his 42 regular season goals and 35 at even-strength led all blueliners, and his 609 shots ranked third, despite missing 21 games with a broken fibula in 2019–20.

In 2020–21, the final year of his contract, Hamilton had 42 points in 55 games, which tied him for seventh among NHL defensemen. Carolina offered him an eight-year extension, but he decided to be the biggest fish in the 2021 free agent market. New Jersey signed him to a seven-year deal worth $63 million, and he scored 17 seconds into his first game on his first shot.

Now 6-foot-6 and 230 pounds, Hamilton has been durable, only sitting out one game over a four-year stretch and one game in 2020–21 after bouncing back from his broken leg. But in 2021–22, he was sidelined for 20 games, including the last 17 with a broken jaw, and the Devils missed the postseason.

Hamilton also lost out on the chance to become the third Olympian in the family when the NHL pulled out of the 2022 Beijing Games. He'll be 32 when the Milano Cortina Olympics open, but he plays a more cerebral than physical game and that ages well.

A gold medal would be a nice addition to the family museum, not to mention the opportunity for the Renaissance man to visit Italy.

Won OHL and CHL Scholastic Player of the Year in 2010–11

Won bronze at the 2012 World Junior Championship

Named OHL and CHL Defenseman of the Year in 2011–12

Tied for NHL lead in goals by a defenseman in 2017–18 (17)

Selected for the 2020 NHL All-Star Game

JACCOB SLAVIN

Hurricanes | Defense | 74

J accob Slavin is the third of Wendi and Robert's five children. Growing up in Erie, Colorado, just north of Denver, he and his siblings — Justin, Jordan, Josiah and Jeremiah — took over the local rink early. At just 2-years-old, Jaccob learned to skate by Pavlovian response, bouncing between strategically placed candy machines on the ice. "He was very motivated by the M&Ms," Wendi remembers fondly.

Jaccob spent summers helping his father out at his auto body shop when he wasn't playing baseball or golfing. His parents put countless miles on their minivan, shuttling their kids, along with foster children they took in, from one sporting venue to another. But hockey won out in the end. His sister, Jordan, played at the University of North Dakota, while Josiah is now

a Chicago Blackhawks prospect and Jeremiah is playing in the United States Hockey League.

That's where Jaccob cut his teeth, with the Chicago Steel starting in 2011. The family had some trepidation with their son moving halfway across the country, but he billeted with a family of faith very similar to his own. "I think that's one of the reasons we connected with him so quickly. He has an ability to connect with everybody," says Jaime Faulkner, who went on to work for the Blackhawks, while her husband, Colin, is in Sales and Marketing with the Chicago Cubs.

A smart, reliable player still growing into his 6-foot-3 frame with the Steel, the Carolina Hurricanes saw that Slavin was just tapping into his full potential and drafted him in the fourth round, 120th overall, in 2012.

Slavin went back to his home state to play two seasons with Colorado College, where he had a team-high 25 points (five goals, 20 assists) in 32 games in 2013–14 to win the National Collegiate Hockey Conference's Rookie of the Year.

In 2015–16 Slavin got his first taste of NHL hockey, and after a handful of games in the American Hockey League, he cemented his spot on the Carolina blue line. He played all 82 games in 2016–17, and he didn't miss a game for the next three seasons.

In 2019, Slavin and wife Kylie adopted Emersyn the day after the Hurricanes' first postseason game in a decade, and she was a good luck charm. Emersyn was born in Washington, and Slavin had nine assists, including three in a 4-3 double-overtime win in Game 7 to upset the defending Stanley Cup champion Washington Capitals. It was two back of the playoff series record of 11 assists jointly held by Paul Coffey and Al MacInnis.

Slavin finished with 11 assists in 15 playoff games in 2019 while jetting back home whenever possible, as Carolina reached the Eastern Conference Final before bowing out to the Boston Bruins.

A steady, calm presence at the back who will never rack up points but will always play the most important minutes, Slavin was named an alternate captain and set a career high with 36 points in 2019–20. The defenseman also got some recognition with his first trip to the NHL All-Star Game.

The following season, Slavin was whistled for just one penalty in 52 games, and that was a delay of game call for putting the puck over the glass. That's unheard of for a defender, especially one who played 23 minutes a night against the opponent's best players, and he became just the fourth defenseman in history to win the Lady Byng Trophy in 2021.

By those standards, Slavin turned into a goon in 2021–22 with 10 penalty minutes in 79 games played, but maybe that was the trade-off for a new career-highs in assists (38) and points (42). Emersyn was rinkside for the Hurricanes' 3-2 win over the Bruins in Game 7 of round one, with her dad earning a pair of assists in 24:03 minutes played. He finished the first round tied

National Collegiate Hockey Conference Rookie of the Year in 2013–14

Played in the 2020 NHL All-Star Game

Won the 2021 Lady Byng Trophy and a finalist in 2022

for the team lead in scoring with eight points and first with a plus-10 rating.

For a promising Canes team in their fourth straight postseason appearance, a second-round exit at the hands of the New York Rangers was a disappointment. During the series, Slavin was announced as a finalist for the Lady Byng for the second straight season, but the Winnipeg Jets' Kyle Connor took home the trophy.

Slavin, who lives in the Raleigh area year-round and is a visible part of his church and community, had more important things to worry about, like teaching his daughter to skate. He used the same M&M incentive he grew up with, but she spent more time sitting down and eating than skating. "She was enjoying her time on the ice," laughed Slavin.

Like father, like daughter.

TRISTAN JARRY

Penguins | Goalie | 35

For those players who spend their whole career fruitlessly chasing the Stanley Cup, Tristan Jarry's ratio of one NHL game played to two championship rings must have been infuriating.

The goaltender is used to staring early. Growing up in North Delta, British Columbia, Jarry was either at the bus stop on his way to hockey practice at 5:30 a.m. or stocking shelves at Jarry's Market, owned by his parents, Michelle and Dave, in South Delta before school.

Coming out of the North Delta Minor Hockey Association and the Delta Hockey Academy, Jarry joined the Western Hockey League's Edmonton Oil Kings when he was 16 and backed up Laurent Brossoit, now with the Vegas Golden Knights, as the Oil Kings won the WHL championship in 2012.

"I had already known that [Jarry] was this next prodigy when he made the team," said Brossoit. "I knew how much better he was than everyone at his age. His presence at that age lit a fire under me to make sure I didn't give him any kind of window of opportunity."

In 2012–13 they split the crease and Jarry went 18-7-0 with a 1.61 goals-against average and .936 save percentage to lead the league in both categories. Despite drafting Matt Murray in 2012, the Pittsburgh Penguins traded up to select Jarry in the second round, 44th overall, in 2013.

The following season Brossoit left for the pros, and Jarry led the Oil Kings to the 2014 WHL and Memorial Cup titles.

Jarry then spent two seasons with Wilkes-Barre/Scranton of the American Hockey League and dressed for two NHL playoff games in 2016. He made his NHL debut in Pittsburgh's regular-season finale in

2017 and was on the bench as Marc-Andre Fleury's backup for the Penguins' first 11 playoff games, until Murray returned from injury. Both years the Penguins won the Stanley Cup.

Fleury left for Vegas in the 2017 expansion draft, and in 2017–18 Jarry backed up Murray. He played in 26 games and led all rookie goalies with 14 wins in 23 starts. He finished with a 14-6-2 record, 2.77 goals-against average, .908 save percentage and two shutouts.

But it was Jarry's AHL partner Casey DeSmith who ended up winning the backup job for the 2018–19 season, sending Jarry back to the AHL for all but two games. He faced a lot of shots behind a mediocre team but thrived with a heavy workload.

Back in the NHL in 2019–20, Jarry went 20-12-1 with a 2.43 goals-against average, .921 save percentage and three shutouts, including a franchise-record shutout streak of 177:15, and earned a spot in the NHL All-Star Game. This convinced the Penguins to trade Murray to the Ottawa Senators in the offseason and sign Jarry to a three-year, $10.5 million contract.

For Jarry, the 2020–21 season will be most remembered for his infamous turnover in overtime versus the New York Islanders in Game 5 of a six-game first round loss. He looked shaky at times in his first postseason as number one, but former goalie and current Penguins general manager Ron Hextall expressed his belief in Jarry, telling him he was still their goalie of the present and future.

The faith was rewarded in 2021–22. Jarry was eighth in the NHL in wins (34) and sixth in goals-against average (2.42) and save percentage (.919). He also played in his second All-Star Game. But he only got into one game in the playoffs, an overtime loss in Game 7 of round one to the New York Rangers after a month off with a broken foot.

Jarry also made headlines in 2022 when the Boston Bruins' Brad Marchand sucker-punched him and then speared him under the mask on his way off the ice, resulting in a six-game suspension for the offender. The rage seemed excessive, even for someone with Marchand's reputation, but apparently "How about that (expletive) save?" from Jarry was enough to set him off.

It was unusual for a taciturn goalie, who coaches usually have to encourage to show more emotion. "That heart rate doesn't get too high," said former Penguins general manager Jim Rutherford. "He's the guy you'd be okay doing surgery on you."

Jarry would just as soon be on his barley farm in Sherwood Park, Alberta, where he gets his early mornings and offseason workouts in before the chores. He likes the solitude and privacy not usually afforded a Canadian with Stanley Cup rings.

He has the jewelry from being on the roster for the two championships, but Jarry's name isn't engraved on the Cup. If this Penguins championship core has another one in them, he'll be the first choice as the last line of defense and the third time will be a charm.

Led the WHL in goals-against average (1.61) and save percentage (.936) in 2012–13

Won the 2014 Memorial Cup with the Edmonton Oil Kings

Won the AHL's Harry "Hap" Holmes Award for fewest goals against (with Casey DeSmith) in 2016–17

Played in two NHL All-Star Games (2020, 2022)

CENTRAL DIVISION

FIRST TEAM

84	**KYLE CONNOR**	Jets	Left Wing
86	**KIRILL KAPRIZOV**	Wild	Left Wing
88	**NATHAN MacKINNON**	Avalanche	Center
90	**ROMAN JOSI**	Predators	Defense
92	**CALE MAKAR**	Avalanche	Defense
94	**JUUSE SAROS**	Predators	Goalie

SECOND TEAM

96	**PATRICK KANE**	Blackhawks	Right Wing
98	**MIKKO RANTANEN**	Avalanche	Right Wing
100	**MARK SCHEIFELE**	Jets	Center
102	**MIRO HEISKANEN**	Stars	Defense
104	**SETH JONES**	Blackhawks	Defense
106	**MARC-ANDRE FLEURY**	Wild	Goalie

TAXI SQUAD

KYLE CONNOR

Jets | Left Wing | 81

When Joe Connor wasn't coaching one of his four kids in youth hockey he was flooding their backyard in Shelby Township. Just north of Detroit, it's where his son Kyle emulated his idol, Red Wings wizard Pavel Datsyuk.

Kyle brought those moves to the Belle Tire program, where one of his teammates was Zach Werenski, now a star defenseman with the Columbus Blue Jackets. In their teens, both tried out for the U.S. National Team Development Program in Ann Arbor. Werenski made it but Connor was cut, so he joined the Youngstown (Ohio) Phantoms of the United States Hockey League when he was 15 instead.

Connor had a chance to show the USNTDP what they missed out on at the 2014 World Under-18

Championship. The rare kid on the team not from the program, he had four goals and seven points in seven games to help Team USA win gold.

In 2014–15, Connor had 34 goals and 80 points in 56 games to lead the USHL and win league MVP, as Youngstown had a record 17-game winning streak. By this time, their top scorer and hardest worker was simply called "Franchise" by management.

With his unmissable numbers and his "jersey-flapping speed," as one NHL scout called it, Connor was drafted 17th overall by the Winnipeg Jets in 2015. He then found his way to Ann Arbor to reunite with Werenski at the University of Michigan.

Connor was one and done as a Wolverine, but couldn't have accomplished much more in his brief matriculation. In 2015–16 he led the NCAA with 35 goals and 71 points in only 38 games. He was the first freshman to score 30 goals since Thomas Vanek in 2002–03, and his 71 points matched Hobey Baker Award-winner Jack Eichel's total the year prior. He won every Big Ten accolade and the Tim Taylor Award as the NCAA's top freshman, but somehow he didn't get the Hobey Baker and was cut from Team USA for the World Junior Championship.

"You have to use it as motivation," said Connor. "There were a bunch of instances where I'd get cut from a team, and you can't sit there and just wonder what could have been, you've got to go out there and work harder."

Hard work and a positive outlook are hallmarks of Connor's hockey life, which he called upon when he was sent down to the Manitoba Moose in the American Hockey League after making the Jets out of his first training camp in 2016.

Connor started the 2017–18 season with the Moose but only lasted four games before the Jets brought him back. He led all NHL rookies with 31 goals, nine more than Calder Trophy winner Mathew Barzal, and he never saw the AHL again.

Connor signed a seven year, $50 million contract in September 2019 and followed that up with his best season to date, scoring 38 goals and 73 points in 71 games of the pandemic-shortened season.

"I would say [he's] quietly become an elite player, right? Because there is more than just putting the puck in the net," said then-head coach Paul Maurice in the 2020 playoff bubble. "This guy, I think he's going to be thought of — he's got a long-term deal so I don't mind saying it — I think he's going to be a top ten player in the National Hockey League."

In terms of putting the puck in the net, Connor is better than top ten. He's sixth in total goals scored since his first full season, just ahead of Nathan Mac-Kinnon, and was tied for fifth in 2021–22 with 47.

Adding 46 assists for 93 points, all career highs, Connor was 18 goals and 23 points ahead of Mark Scheifele, his closest teammate. It earned him a trip to his first All-Star Game and with only four penalty minutes all season, the fewest among the league's top 100 scorers, he won the Lady Byng Trophy for sportsmanship and gentlemanly conduct.

Playing in one of the NHL's smaller markets, the Jet still flies under the radar, but for those in the know he's got a few things in common with another Connor, two provinces over.

"His speed is electric. Like, he's not far off from McDavid," according to former Jets assistant coach Todd Woodcroft.

"K.C. can score on a breakaway. K.C. can score on a goal-line jam. K.C. can score coming off the half wall, he can tip it," added Woodcroft. "That guy is a scoring chance waiting to happen."

Won gold at the 2014 World Under-18 Championship

Named USA Hockey Junior Player of the Year in 2014–15

Led the NCAA in goals (35) and points (71) and won the Tim Taylor award as Top Collegiate Rookie in 2015–16

Played in the 2022 All-Star Game

2022 Lady Byng Trophy winner

KIRILL KAPRIZOV

Wild | Left Wing | 97

If NHL success is measured in nicknames, Kirill Kaprizov is off to a solid start.

He came into the NHL with "Kirill the Thrill" and it didn't take long to be popularized. Minnesota Wild play-by-play announcer Anthony LaPanta used it when Kaprizov scored the overtime winner in his NHL debut against the Los Angeles Kings on January 2021, five and a half long years after he was drafted (with a few extra months wait thanks to the pandemic).

Kaprizov is from Novokuznetsk in Siberia, an industrial city of 500,000 people that's closer to Mongolia than Moscow. Maybe that's why he was still available when Minnesota chose him in the fifth round, 135th overall, in 2015. It was a prescient pick, and over the next few years it started to look downright genius.

In 2017, Kaprizov was captain of the bronze medal-winning World Junior Championship team and broke Russia's tournament record with nine goals in seven games. A year later, the 20-year-old was the youngest player on the Olympic Athletes from Russia team. He played on a line with Detroit Red Wings legend Pavel Datsyuk, who raved about the experience, and scored the "golden goal" in overtime at the 2018 PyeongChang Olympics. A year after that, Kaprizov led the KHL in goals, set a single-season record with 11 game-winners, and won the 2019 Golden Stick as regular season MVP and the Gagarin Cup as a member of CSKA Moscow.

The following year, Kaprizov led the KHL in goals again but couldn't defend the championship because the playoffs were canceled due to COVID. Over those two seasons, he became the youngest player in KHL history to reach the 100-goal mark, played in his fourth and fifth KHL All-Star Games and was widely regarded as the best player not in the NHL.

Starting his first NHL season at 23 after his KHL contract expired, and following some contract complications due to the NHL's hiatus and return to play, Kaprizov showed up with huge expectations from Wild fans and some culture shock to navigate in the middle of a pandemic.

The pressure didn't show. Not only did Kaprizov become the first Wild player to record three points in his first NHL game, he was just the third player in history and first since 1990 to score an overtime winner in his NHL debut. Two months later, teammate Matt Dumba bestowed upon him the "Dollar Dollar Bill Kirill" nickname — "Dollar Bill" for short. He even made t-shirts for the team with Kaprizov wearing shades with dollar signs on them. Because he was already money.

Kaprizov lived up to the moniker, leading all rookies with 27 goals and 51 points in 55 regular-season games. He was also first on the Wild in scoring,

Led the 2017 World Junior Championship in goals (9) and points (12) and named Best Forward

Led the 2018 Olympics with five goals and won gold with the Olympic Athletes from Russia

Won the 2019 Gagarin Cup and Golden Stick as KHL MVP

Won the 2021 Calder Trophy

Played in the 2022 All-Star Game

Set Wild franchise records in goals (47), assists (61) and points (108) in 2021–22

making him just the fourth rookie in the past two decades to lead his team in scoring.

It earned Kaprizov the Calder Trophy, the first in Wild history, and it was one vote shy of unanimous. That was just an appetizer, which he may have had too many of while quarantining in Florida on the eve of the season and showing up a little "chunky," by coach Dean Evason's estimation.

Kaprizov didn't score a goal in his first eight games in 2021–22 but quickly got in game shape and took off. He ended up fifth in the NHL in both goals (47) and points (108), two points ahead of Hart Trophy-nominee Auston Matthews and two behind former Hart-winner Leon Draisaitl. With 61 assists, he set single-season franchise records in all three categories, while the Wild set team records with 53 wins and 113 points.

Kaprizov set or tied 12 different franchise records in 2021–22, which included a series record seven goals in a six game, first round loss to the St. Louis Blues. He also had the first hat trick in Wild playoff history, which prompted a less traditional bra being thrown on the ice among the hats.

That speaks to Kaprizov's appeal among a rabid Wild fanbase that's been starved of real star power, at least the game-breaking type on the offensive end. His boundless enthusiasm and sense of humor endear him to fans and advertisers alike. Even with the language barrier, which is fading, he had a North American-wide "Dollar Bill" commercial for Great Clips.

"He's popular. He's going to be a star. He's great for the market. He's great for shifting the perception of our team," says Wild general manager Bill Guerin. "But the bottom line is that we want to win more games than we lose. We want to win a championship. And he's going to be a big piece of that puzzle."

NATHAN MacKINNON

There must be something in the water in Cole Harbour, Nova Scotia, a town of about 25,000 residents and probably the highest quotient of hockey talent per capita on the planet. Not only did the town produce Sidney Crosby, one of the best players to ever grace NHL ice, but it also gave the world Nathan MacKinnon.

MacKinnon put skates on at just 2 years old, and by 14 he had outgrown the local hockey scene. With a successful template in place, he left Cole Harbour to attend Shattuck-St. Mary's in Minnesota, just like Crosby did.

After two years at boarding school, MacKinnon came home to play for the Quebec Major Junior Hockey League's Halifax Mooseheads, about 10 miles west of Cole Harbour. He led the Mooseheads to their first Memorial Cup in 2013, scoring seven goals and six assists in four games to take home the Stafford Smythe Trophy as tournament MVP.

Another Cole Harbour quality is the ability to rise to the occasion. Against the Portland Winterhawks and Seth Jones, the top-ranked skater in the upcoming entry draft, MacKinnon had a hat trick in a win in the preliminary round. Facing them again in the final, he had another hat trick, including an empty-netter to clinch the title.

The Colorado Avalanche picked MacKinnon first overall in 2013, and he was 18 years and 31 days old on his NHL debut, making him the youngest player in franchise history. He finished the 2013–14 season leading all rookies in assists (39) and points (63) and tied for most goals (24). He also had three assists in the first game of the postseason to become the first rookie in history to accomplish that feat in his playoff debut. He capped the season off by becoming the youngest player to ever win the Calder Trophy.

The next few seasons were a little bleak, despite

MacKinnon's best efforts. He led the last place Avalanche in scoring in 2016–17 and was their only representative at the 2017 NHL All-Star Game, but Colorado missed the playoffs for the third straight year.

In 2017–18, things began to turn. MacKinnon jumped to fifth in the NHL in scoring with 97 points and the Avalanche made the playoffs for the first time since 2014. A year later, he was tied for sixth in goals (41) and seventh in points (99), one point behind Crosby, and he took it to another level in the 2019 postseason.

MacKinnon had 13 points in 12 playoff games, and several of his six goals were of the did-you-just-see-that variety, but the Avalanche fell to the San Jose Sharks in the second round.

It became a recurring theme. MacKinnon had 93 points in only 69 games in 2019–20 and won the Lady Byng Trophy, but the Avalanche lost in the official second round of the playoff bubble in 2020 to the Dallas Stars, and then again in 2021 to the Vegas Golden Knights. After the latter loss, a visibly upset and raw MacKinnon said, "I've been in the league nine years and haven't won sh*t."

It was team-wide motivation for a very talented Avalanche in 2021–22. MacKinnon had 32 goals and 88 points in 65 games and finished the season with 648 career points, sixth in the NHL since he entered the league.

After sweeping the Predators in the first round, a breathtaking end-to-end rush by MacKinnon in Game 5 of the second round made him the first player in franchise history to score a hat trick in a potential series-clinching game. After the highlight of the playoffs, however, the St. Louis Blues tied the game and won in overtime.

Collars tightened when another second round loss looked possible, but the Avalanche finished them off and then swept the Edmonton Oilers in a much-anticipated MacKinnon vs. (Connor) McDavid matchup in the Western Conference Final.

Facing the two-time defending champion Tampa Bay Lightning next, MacKinnon had six points in the six-game series, including a goal and an assist in the clincher, as Colorado won its first title since 2001. He led the team with 13 goals and had 24 points in 20 playoff games.

With as much emotion as a year prior, a euphoric MacKinnon was interviewed on the ice after lifting the Cup. Asked about the upcoming Stanley Cup celebration back home, he noted the good omen that his hotel number in Tampa the night before ended in Crosby's 87 and said: "I've been the drunkest guy at two of his, so he better be the drunkest guy at mine."

They're going to need to drink some water in Cole Harbour.

- Named Memorial Cup MVP in 2013
- Won the 2014 Calder Trophy, the youngest player ever to win it
- Won gold at the 2015 World Championship
- Won the 2020 Lady Byng Trophy
- Three-time Hart Trophy finalist
- Named to five NHL All-Star Games (2017, 2018, 2019, 2020, 2022)
- 2022 Stanley Cup champion

ROMAN JOSI

Predators | Defense | 59

Nashville Predators defenseman Roman Josi played forward until he was 14, and only two years after moving back to the blue line the native of Bern, Switzerland, joined SC Bern in the country's top division. It takes elite talent to ascend that quickly, which he has in his DNA.

"My mother was a swimmer on the national team, and my father was a top-level footballer," explained Josi. "When I first started, I didn't really mind how I played. It wasn't that important. But when the first agents started to show up, I was 15, and I realized that hockey was big business."

The Predators drafted Josi in the second round, 38th overall, in 2008, and made his NHL debut in the 2011–12 season. By his second year, he was already on the team's top pairing. He followed that season up by leading the underdog Swiss to the 2013 World Championship final against host Sweden. He had Switzerland's only goal in the final, one of his four goals and nine points in the tournament, and took home the top defenseman and MVP awards to go with his silver medal.

When captain and franchise icon Shea Weber was traded in 2016, Josi took on the roles of shutdown defender and defensive anchor that his former partner had held. He emerged from Weber's shadow and started getting the recognition he deserved, although he's so positionally and fundamentally sound that he doesn't always stand out — he's just efficient, effective and complete.

Averaging more ice time than anyone on the team in 2016–17, Josi helped the Predators squeak into the playoffs as the eighth seed and then sweep the top-seeded Chicago Blackhawks on the way to the franchise's first Western Conference championship and trip to the Stanley Cup Final. He had six goals and 14 points in 22 playoff games, which was second on the team and among NHL defensemen in scoring.

When Mike Fisher retired after the season, it was an easy decision for coaches and management to stitch the C on Josi's sweater. He's taken leadership in his long stride — on the ice and in the community — while continuing to add dimensions to his game, notably on the offensive end.

In the shortened 2019–20 season, Josi set career highs in goals (16), assists (49) and points (65) to set Predators' franchise records for assists and points by a defenseman in a season. He finished first among NHL defensemen in shots (260), second in points and assists, tied for second in goals, third in average time on ice (25:47), and fifth in powerplay points (23). He was the only defenseman with at least 15 goals, 45 assists, 60 points, a +20 rating and 25:00 of average ice

time, and he led in zone exits, zone entries, and offensive-zone puck possession time.

It wasn't a shock when Josi took home his first Norris Trophy in 2020. He's the first Swiss-born player to win a major NHL award, and in April 2021 he recorded his 435th career point to pass his idol and friend Mark Streit for the most points by a Swiss-born player in NHL history.

In 2021–22 Josi started to put that record out of reach with a season for the ages at age 31. He set a Predators team scoring record and led all NHL defensemen with 96 points, 10 points ahead of second place Cale Makar and his nearest teammate, and tied for 11th among all skaters. He was the first defenseman to hit the 90-point milestone since Ray Bourque in 1993–94.

At one point late in the season, Josi had 24 assists and 28 points over a 13-game scoring streak to put Nashville on his back and bring them to the playoffs for the eighth season in a row.

Josi was named a finalist for the Norris Trophy and the Ted Lindsay Award, which is given to the most

Won silver at the 2013 and 2018 World Championship
Named best defender and MVP of the 2013 World Championship
Played in four NHL All-Star Games (2016, 2019, 2020, 2022)
Won the 2020 Norris Trophy
Led all NHL defensemen in assists (73) and points (96) in 2021–22
Finalist for the Norris Trophy and Ted Lindsay Award in 2022

outstanding player as voted by their peers. Nominated alongside Connor McDavid and Auston Matthews, the last defenseman to win it was Bobby Orr in 1975.

Josi came oh-so close to 100 points, which likely would have clinched both trophies for him and made him the first since Brian Leetch in 1991–92. The five defensemen in NHL history to reach triple digits are all in the Hall of Fame — Leetch, Paul Coffey, Al MacInnis, Orr and Denis Potvin.

Even if Josi never gets to 100, and he has six more years on his contract to try, becoming the first Swiss player to reach the Hall and hockey's highest honor is money in the bank.

CALE MAKAR

Avalanche | Defense | 8

C ale Makar has been blessed by the hockey gods with skills that run the gamut of the game and almost never coalesce in one individual player.

Chosen by the Medicine Hat Tigers in the eighth round of the 2013 Western Hockey League draft, Makar was 125 pounds and a long shot. He and his family decided the college route was best for him anyway, so the pint-sized defenseman left his Calgary home and joined the Brooks Bandits of the Alberta Junior Hockey League late in the 2014–15 season.

"He looked like someone's little brother on the ice," according to Bandits coach Ryan Papaioannou, but he could skate and handle the puck like few others. In 157 combined regular-season and playoff games, Makar had 44 goals and 172 points, while adding a sneaky physicality to his game.

After winning gold at the 2015 World Junior A Challenge, NHL buzz started to spread, and Makar's stock skyrocketed with AJHL and Western Canada Cup victories.

The Colorado Avalanche drafted Makar fourth overall in 2017, and he then went to the University of Massachusetts as planned, where he had 21 points in 34 games. He also led the 2018 World Junior tournament in goals (3) and points (8) by a defenseman to help Canada take gold.

The Avalanche wanted Makar to join the team in 2018, but he chose to go back for his sophomore season to work on his game. He had 33 assists and 49 points in 41 games to lead UMass to its first Frozen Four and won the 2019 Hobey Baker Award as the best men's player in the NCAA.

But that was just a prelude. Makar signed a contract with the Avalanche hours after UMass lost the national title game and was parachuted into the playoffs a day later, on April 15, 2019. He scored in the first period of his first game against his childhood favorites, the Calgary Flames. It held up as the game-winner and made him the first defenseman to score a playoff goal in his NHL debut.

In his rookie year, Makar had 38 assists and 50 points in 57 games, added 15 points in 15 playoff games, and won the 2020 Calder Trophy. And after getting 36 assists and 44 points in 44 games in his second season to finish just behind Adam Fox for the 2021 Norris Trophy, he signed a six-year, $54 million contract with the Avalanche.

For those east of the Rockies somehow unaware of him, 2021–22 was the season of Makar. He had one of the highlights of the year with a jaw-dropping spin-o-rama, top-shelf backhand overtime winner against Marc-Andre Fleury and the Chicago Black-hawks, and there'd be so much more to come.

Makar set the goal-scoring record by an Avalanche/ Quebec Nordiques defenseman with 28, and his 86 points were second among NHL defensemen and broke Steve Duchesne's franchise mark of 82 for the Nordiques in 1992–93.

In the playoffs, Makar became the first defenseman in NHL history with five points in a series-clinching game when he had a goal and four assists in a 6-5 win against the Edmonton Oilers in Game 4 of the Western Conference Final. Only Wayne Gretzky and John Anderson have had more. It tied an Avalanche record at any position, and he was the eighth player in NHL history to put his team into the Stanley Cup Final with five points, and the second-youngest after Maurice Richard in 1944.

Makar had three goals and seven points in the Final, while accepting the Norris Trophy during the series, and finished third among all skaters with 21 assists and 29 points in 20 playoff games, a 119-point pace over the regular season. Only Hall of Fame defensemen Paul Coffey, Brian Leetch and Al MacInnis had more.

ESPN's Emily Kaplan asked captain Gabriel Landeskog what other teams might learn from the Avalanche's championship run. "Find a Cale Makar somewhere," he replied.

Makar was the unanimous choice for the Conn Smythe Trophy, joining seven-time Norris Trophy winner Nicklas Lidstrom and Bobby Orr as the only players in NHL history to win the Norris, Conn Smythe and Stanley Cup in the same season.

With 60 points in 55 career postseason games, Makar only trails Orr among defensemen in points-per-game in NHL playoff history. "The closest player we've ever seen offensively and defensively that can make an impact on the game that much — probably Bobby Orr," said Gretzky of Makar during the postseason.

The hockey world had witnessed the birth of a legend, and the 23-year-old Makar was already skating among the immortals.

Won gold at the 2018 World Junior Championship
Won the Hobey Baker Award in 2019
Won the Calder Trophy in 2020
Played in the 2022 NHL All-Star Game
Won the Norris Trophy in 2022
Won the Stanley Cup and Conn Smythe Trophy in 2022

JUUSE SAROS

Predators | Goalie | 74

On February 24, 2022, the Nashville Predators retired the first number in franchise history. Juuse Saros watched as Pekka Rinne's 35 rose to the rafters of Bridgestone Arena and then went out and stopped 27 shots in regulation and four more in a shootout as the Predators beat the Dallas Stars 2-1.

Nashville has a knack for unearthing Finnish gems. Rinne, an eighth-round pick, has every franchise record, as well as the most games played, victories and shutouts by a Finnish goalie in NHL history. They did it again when they chose Saros in the fourth round, 99th overall, in 2013, a selection that looked even smarter a year later.

Playing for HPK in his hometown of Hameenlinna in 2013–14, Saros appeared in 44 of 60 regular season games with a .923 save percentage and a 1.76 goals-against average to be named Liiga Rookie of the Year. He would have played even more, but he was busy at the World Junior Championship, winning gold and being named to the tournament all-star team after leading the tournament in save percentage (.943) and goals-against average (1.57).

Saros celebrated that with a summer of mandatory military service, putting on-ice accomplishments in perspective. "When I'm in a slump, I remind myself of the fact there's more to life than hockey," said a young Saros. "The mental side is probably the most important thing in goaltending."

Another life lesson was in demystifing your heroes. When Saros first arrived in Nashville, he moved in with Rinne. "We're living in this big house and going to the practice with these guys that you grew up watching on TV," remembered Saros. "So yeah, it was all kind of bizarre."

The two bonded and shared a room on the road, even though they were fighting for the same job. "I think we both realize that we've tried to separate the off-ice and on-ice thing," said Rinne. "It's not the same. We still battle and we compete. I want to play, and he wants to play. It's a healthy situation, but then off the ice he's like a little brother to me. He's very close to me."

It wasn't much of a competition at first. After Saros beat Marc-Andre Fleury, his other goaltending idol growing up, for his first NHL win, he spent much of the next two seasons with the Milwaukee Admirals of the American Hockey League. Even when he had extended stays in the NHL he struggled to be consistent, while Rinne won the 2018 Vezina Trophy.

It wasn't until 2020 that student started to surpass the teacher. In the playoff bubble, Saros ended Rinne's streak of 89 straight playoff games started, and after the Predators drafted goalie Yaroslav Askarov with the 11th overall pick in the offseason, creating even more competition, Saros responded.

It wasn't immediate, but after a 3-4-0 record, .880 save percentage and a 3.66 goals-against average in the first month, Saros set career highs in starts (35), wins (21), save percentage (.927), and goals-against average (2.28). Down the stretch he went 16-6-1 and led the NHL in save percentage (.939) from March 1 to get the Predators into the postseason. He then tied and broke franchise records for saves in a playoff game with 52 and 58 in consecutive games.

You typically need to be at least 6-feet-tall to get on the modern NHL goalie ride, but the 5-foot-11 Saros isn't your typical goalie. Though he's undersized he thrives on a heavy workload. The Predators may have pushed that in 2021–22, however. He led the NHL in games started and played (67), faced the second-most shots (2,107), made the second-most saves (1,934) and led in ice time (3,931:23).

Saros finished 38-25-3, third in wins, tied for sixth in shutouts (four), eighth in save percentage (.918), and tied for 15th in goals-against-average (2.64), but missed the end of the season and the playoffs with an ankle injury. Not surprisingly, the Predators were swept in the first round without the main reason they got there.

As then-Dallas coach Rick Bowness said when Saros stole the game on Rinne's big night, "We deserved two. We outplayed them. Their goalie was the difference in the game."

It was a familiar refrain from opponents as Saros played in his first All-Star Game and was a finalist for the Vezina Trophy. He has a few more awards and records to collect to equal his former roommate, but he doesn't mind playing in the long shadow cast by the number hanging above him.

Won gold at the 2014 World Junior Championship with tournament bests in goals-against average (1.57) and save percentage (.943)

Liiga Rookie of the Year in 2014

Won silver medals at the 2014 and 2016 World Championships

Named to the NHL All-Rookie Team in 2017–18

Played in the 2022 All-Star Game

First in the NHL in games played (67) and third in wins (38) in 2021–22

PATRICK KANE

Blackhawks | Right Wing | 88

record in his second season with 102 points in 58 games. In 2006–07, his lone season in the Ontario Hockey League, he had 62 goals and 145 points in 58 games for the London Knights. He was both the Canadian Hockey League's leading scorer and Rookie of the Year.

After being drafted first overall by the Chicago Blackhawks in 2007, Kane stepped right into the NHL and had 21 goals and 72 points to win the Calder Trophy. It was the Blackhawks' first winning season in six years and the start of a resurgence that culminated in three Stanley Cups.

In 2010 Kane had 10 goals and 28 points in 22 playoff games, the last of which in Game 6 against the Philadelphia Flyers made him the youngest player to score the Stanley Cup–winning goal in overtime.

Kane's nine goals and 19 points in the 2013 play-offs earned him the Conn Smythe Trophy as the Blackhawks brought another championship back to Chicago, and in 2015 he came back from a broken collarbone to score 23 points in 23 playoff games to win his third Stanley Cup.

But troubled times were ahead. In August 2015 Kane was accused of sexual assault at his lake house outside of Buffalo. While the district attorney declined to press charges, it wasn't forgotten in opposing rinks, especially in his hometown.

Kane had already pleaded guilty to noncriminal disorderly conduct as a result of assaulting a cab driver in 2009, and the people of Buffalo had run out of patience with their wayward child and weren't afraid to voice it when the Blackhawks came to town.

Either Kane is adept at compartmentalizing or the anger directed at him was motivation in 2015–16. He had a 26-game point streak and in his lone game in Buffalo he tied the score with 35.9 seconds left and then beat the Sabres with a shootout goal.

After leading the NHL that season with 106 points (46 goals, 60 assists), 17 more than second-place Jamie

P atrick Kane is the product of working-class South Buffalo, where there's a "special culture," according to NHL icon Scotty Bowman, former coach and general manager of the Sabres. "If you're from South Buffalo — or you're accepted there — you're a different kind of guy."

Generously listed at 5-foot-10 and 177 pounds now, Kane was always the smallest and usually the best on his team. By the age of 11, he was putting up 230 points in a 60-game season. At 14 he had 160 points in 70 games for the Detroit HoneyBaked AAA team. Twice cut by the U.S. National Team Development Program because of his size, Kane broke a program

Benn, Kane became the first American-born player to win the Art Ross and Hart trophies. He completed the hat trick with the Ted Lindsay Award.

These are a few of the reasons why in 2017 Kane was named one of the NHL's 100 Greatest Players ever, one of only six active players to make the list, and he continues to pad his résumé.

After leading the 2018 World Championship in scoring with 20 points in 10 games and being named MVP, Kane had 44 goals and career highs in assists (66) and points (110) in 2018–19. He was third in NHL scoring and a finalist for the Ted Lindsay Award.

His skill is undeniable, but one of the reasons Kane has and will continue to put up these numbers is another Gretzky-esque quality — elusiveness. Already slender and shifty like the Great One, he now focuses on flexibility and mobility instead of strength.

It's paid off. In 2021–22, at the ripe age of 33, he tied his own career high and was sixth in the NHL with 66 assists, and had the third-highest point total of his career with 92. Since entering the league 15 years ago, Kane's 750 assists lead all players and he's third in

Won the Calder Trophy in 2008
Played in nine NHL All-Star Games (2009, 2011, 2012, 2015, 2016, 2017, 2018, 2019, 2020)
Won the Stanley Cup three times (2010, 2013, 2015)
Voted the Conn Smythe Trophy winner in 2013
Won the Hart Trophy, Art Ross Trophy and Ted Lindsay Award in 2016

total points at 1,180, trailing only Alex Ovechkin and Sidney Crosby.

Kane's esteem among his contemporaries is as high as the company he keeps. In a 2022 NHL Players' Association poll, he was voted best stickhandler by 57.3 percent, up 7.9 percent from the year prior and well ahead of one Connor McDavid at 22.8 percent.

"When I was able to win the Ted Lindsay Award in 2016, I thought that was almost better recognition than the Hart because it's voted on by the players," said Kane. "To hear that from my peers, it's very special, considering it's coming from the best players in the world."

MIKKO RANTANEN

Avalanche | Right Wing | 96

Mikko Rantanen is the first NHL player from Nousiainen, a small town in the southwest of Finland. It might be why he flew under the radar, even in that hockey-mad country.

At 16, the 5-foot-10, 175-pound Rantanen joined TPS Turku in Liiga, Finland's top flight. Two years and six inches of height later, the 18-year-old was named an alternate captain and was second on the team in scoring and won the Ville Peltonen Award as the league's playoff MVP.

Rantanen wasn't a marquee name in the 2015 draft class, which gave the NHL Connor McDavid and Jack Eichel, but the 10th overall pick by the Colorado Avalanche made the team out of training camp. He played nine games at the start of the 2015–16 season before being sent down to the American Hockey League's

San Antonio Rampage. There he had 24 goals and 60 points in 52 games and was named AHL co-Rookie of the Year.

Taking a midseason break, Rantanen returned home to play in the 2016 World Juniors. He scored a goal against the Russians in the final as the Finns won gold on home soil, but even as captain he didn't receive the same coverage as teammates Patrik Laine, Sebastian Aho and Jesse Puljujarvi.

Rantanen finished the season with a silver at the World Championship and started the next in Colorado. His growth spurt meant he was still a bit "clumsy," according to linemate Nathan MacKinnon, when he entered the NHL. But in 2017–18, his second full season, he finished second on the team to MacKinnon and tied for 16th in the NHL with

84 points — the most by a Finnish-born player since Teemu Selanne and Olli Jokinen in 2006–07.

The following season, Rantanen came out blazing. He had 16 assists and 21 points in 12 games in October 2018 and was the first player to reach the 30-, 40- and 50-point marks. He was the second Avalanche player to have the NHL scoring lead at Christmas, after Hall of Famer Peter Forsberg, and his 59 points were the most by anyone at the holiday break since Sidney Crosby had 60 in 2010–11.

During the 2018 calendar year, Rantanen had the second-most points (113) of any player, behind McDavid (121), and his 79 assists led the NHL.

Still just 22, Rantanen cooled off a little in the second half and missed the last eight games of the regular season with an upper-body injury. He finished with 87 points in 74 games and led the club with 16 power-play goals, tied for sixth in the NHL and the most by an Avalanche player since Joe Sakic in 2006–07. In the playoffs he added six goals and 14 points in 12 games.

Now 6-foot-4 and 215 pounds, Rantanen could play the physical game, but he's still the skinny kid who learned to play with vision and a high hockey IQ. "He's so big and he's so strong," says MacKinnon. "He's definitely a freak off the ice."

Rantanen signed a six-year, $55.5-million extension in 2019, and in 2020–21 he led the Avalanche and was fifth in the NHL in goals (30) and tied for fifth in points (66). He was also first in the NHL with a plus-30 rating and received votes for both the Hart and Selke Trophies.

In 2021–22, Rantanen led the Avalanche again with 36 goals and 92 points, both career highs. On a team with McKinnon, captain Gabriel Landeskog and all-world defenseman Cale Makar, that's no small feat.

Rantanen didn't score a goal until the Avalanche's eighth game of the 2022 postseason, but then he had 14 points over an eight-game streak that included a goal in every game of a sweep over the Edmonton Oilers in the Western Conference Final. He finished with 20 assists and 25 points in 20 games, second on the Avalanche to Conn Smythe Trophy winner Makar and fifth among all playoff performers.

Even-keeled Rantanen is an even point-a-game player with 408 points in 408 career regular season games, behind only McDavid (697) and Mitch Marner (455) from the class of 2015. In the playoffs Rantanen is first, with 77 points in 63 games. He'd be significantly lower in recognition score and column inches, but he's the only one from the deep first round of the draft with a Stanley Cup ring.

"I honestly think it's mind blowing how it's taken everybody so long to recognize what he's been able to do in this league," says Landeskog.

Captained Finland to gold at the 2016 World Junior Championship

Shared the 2016 Dudley "Red" Garret Memorial Trophy as AHL rookie of the year

Won silver at the 2016 World Championship

Played in the 2019 NHL All-Star Game

Led the NHL with a plus-30 in 2020–21

2022 Stanley Cup champion

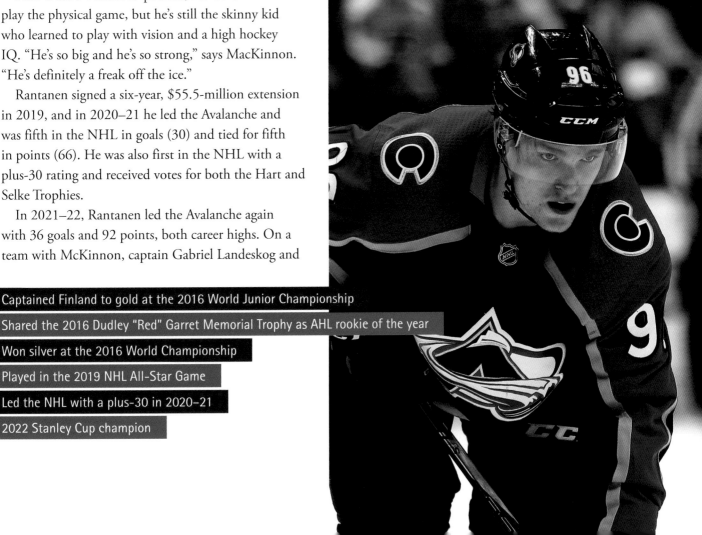

MARK SCHEIFELE

Jets | Center | 55

Growing up in Kitchener, Ontario, Mark Scheifele was passionate about hockey and sports obsessed. "He would sit in this big white chair in the living room, eating his cereal as he was watching SportsCentre," said his father, Brad.

All three Scheifele kids played sports, but Mark was the most serious and the most competitive. "I was always the worst loser," he recalled. "Anytime I lost it was a big ordeal . . . I just couldn't stand for losing."

The drive was inborn, not taught. The Scheifele parents insisted their children play multiple sports and have fun in each of them. Mark played hockey, soccer, lacrosse, volleyball and track and field, and he left a trail of broken equipment when things didn't go his way. Never his precious hockey sticks, though.

Scheifele didn't focus on hockey until he was 16. He was chosen in the seventh round of the Ontario Hockey League draft by the Saginaw Spirit in 2009 but was sent home after training camp.

Back in Kitchener with the Junior B Dutchmen, Scheifele had 55 points in 51 games and was the league's rookie of the year. His OHL rights were then acquired by the Barrie Colts, where coach Dale Hawerchuk — Winnipeg's first overall draft pick in 1981, a former Jets captain and a Hall of Fame inductee — convinced him to learn and grow under his tutelage.

The Colts finished last in the OHL in 2010–11, but Scheifele had 75 points in 66 games and climbed into the low first round in NHL draft rankings. A few eyebrows were raised when the Jets picked him seventh overall in 2011, their first selection after the franchise had relocated from Atlanta. Management knew he wasn't going to stroll right into the NHL as an 18-year-old, but they believed he had the work ethic to get there and the humility to realize he'd need it.

Scheifele's first NHL game was also the reborn Jets' first since returning to Manitoba, and his first goal came four games later, in front of family in Toronto, against the Maple Leafs on October 19, 2011. It was his only point with the Jets before he was sent back to Barrie, where he had 142 points in 92 games over two seasons.

In 2013–14 Scheifele stuck with the Jets permanently, and in 2016, after inheriting the first-line role, Scheifele showed what he was truly capable of. In 82 games between January 2016 and January 2017, his 85 points trailed only Sidney Crosby and Connor McDavid.

After Scheifele finished 2016–17 with 32 goals and 82 points, good for seventh in the league, he was limited to 60 games in 2017–18. He still managed to get 60 points, and he picked that pace up in the postseason, with 14 goals and 20 points in 17 playoff games as the Jets made it to the Western Conference Final. Along the way Scheifele set records for most away goals in a single series, with seven against the Nashville Predators, and most away goals in one postseason, with 11.

Back to a full schedule in 2018–19, Scheifele had career-highs with 38 goals and 84 points, and after five points in six postseason games, Kitchener Clutch had 36 goals and 80 points in 70 career playoff games in the OHL, AHL and NHL.

Scheifele played in his second All-Star Game in 2020, and he was tied for sixth in the NHL in assists (42) and ninth in points (63) in the shortened and realigned 2020–21 season.

In the final of the all-Canadian North Division, Scheifele's passion for winning — or hatred of losing — went too far. He laid a late and dangerous hit on Montreal's Jake Evans after Evans sealed the Canadiens' Game 1 win with an empty-netter. Wild-eyed and incredulous immediately afterwards, he eventually accepted his punishment.

Scheifele received a four-game suspension that effectively ended the Jets' chances of advancing. They were swept, so the final game carried over to the 2021–22 season, and so did his frustration.

After missing the last nine games of the season with a shoulder injury, Scheifele finished second in team scoring with 29 goals and 70 points, the sixth straight season he's been a point-per-game player, but his defensive commitment was questioned at times. The deep Jets lineup underachieved, and he simmered throughout.

"It's one of those years you look back on and some of it's a blur and some of it's really clear. It's definitely a year I'll try to forget a little bit," said Scheifele. "But like I said before you can't dwell on it too long, you have to reflect and think about the good and the bad and the ugly and come back better next year."

Won bronze at the 2012 World Junior Championship

Won gold at the 2016 World Championship

Won silver at the 2017 World Championship

Finished seventh in NHL scoring (82 points) in 2016–17 and ninth (63 points) in 2020–21

Played in two NHL All-Star Games (2019, 2020)

MIRO HEISKANEN

Stars | Defense | 4

After leading all players in assists (10) and defensemen in points (12) at the 2017 Under-18 World Championship, Heiskanen was named the tournament's Best Defenseman. He then became the youngest defenseman in the history of Finland's Liiga to score four or more game-winning goals and won the 2018 Pekka Rautakallio Award as the league's Best Defenseman. He also represented Finland at the 2018 World Junior Championship, PyeongChang Olympics and World Championship.

"It's his maturity," said Dallas general manager Jim Nill during Heiskanen's first NHL training camp in 2018. "Who he is off the ice is who he is on the ice. He just turned 19 but he conducts himself like a man. He did that over in Europe last year. When you go watch him play, you understand why. He can slow the game down and 99 percent of the time he makes the right play, he doesn't overdo it. He has a very calming demeanour on the back end."

Heiskanen had 33 points in 2018–19 while playing all 82 games and leading rookie defensemen with 12 goals and 182 shots on goal and all rookies with 23:07 in average ice time. He also tied for third among rookies with four game-winning goals, setting a franchise record for first-year defenseman, and became the second-youngest player in team history to play in the All-Star Game.

In the 2019–20 season, Heiskanen had career highs in assists (27) and points (35) and received votes for both the Lady Byng and Norris Trophies, but it was in the strange gauntlet of the postseason bubble in Edmonton that he showed the full scope of his powers. After 16 games he had 21 points, making him one of eight defensemen with 21 points in 16 games or fewer in a single postseason. The other seven, including Orr, are now in the Hall of Fame.

Heiskanen finished with 26 points in 27 games, tops among all defensemen, and would have been a heavy favourite for the Conn Smythe Trophy if the Stars

C hoosing Bobby Orr's number 4 is a bold choice for a defenseman, and while there may never be another Orr, Miro Heiskanen's skill set makes him a reasonable Finnish facsimile. He glides more than he skates, exudes an effortless calm, and his stickhandling, vision and passing make zone exits and entries look easy.

Born in 1999 in Espoo, Heiskanen missed Orr by a couple decades, but they also shared the child prodigy label. Drafted third overall by the Dallas Stars in 2017 out of Helsinki's HIFK, he'd already accomplished just about everything he could on the ice before he hit legal drinking age in Finland.

had beaten the Tampa Bay Lightning in the Stanley Cup Final.

Heiskanen proved he can put up prodigious numbers but his first focus is in his own end. In 2021–22, he was on Dallas' top two defensive pairs — teamed with Esa Lindell, he was first in expected goals against per 60 minutes, and when he played with Ryan Suter, he was second. He was also ahead of all three Norris finalists in expected goals prevented over the course of the season.

After playing in 257 of 260 possible games in the age of COVID, Heiskanen got mononucleosis in March 2022 and missed 11 games. Without him the Stars dropped in every defensive category,

Won gold (2016) and silver (2017) at the Under-18 World Championship

Won the 2018 Pekka Rautakallio Award as Liiga's Best Defenseman

Named to the 2018–19 NHL All-Rookie Team

Played in the 2019 NHL All-Star Game

Led all defensemen with 26 points in the 2020 NHL playoffs

including 15 spots among NHL teams in high-danger shots allowed and 20 in expected goals allowed.

But it's not all defense; the Stars' five-on-five offense was nine percent above the NHL average with him on the ice and two percent below without him.

Heiskanen was supposed to be limited to about 15 minutes in his first game back from mono but he played 20. "Talking to him after, he's looking at me like, 'Give me more,'" said then-head coach Rick Bowness. "It's typical Miro."

The next game he led all players with 27:23.

An award for defenders, the Norris Trophy tends to be given to the player who creates the most offense. It's hard to imagine there isn't one in the future for Heiskanen, however, who's trusted in all situations, plays against the opponent's top line, elevates everyone around him, and has taken on the role of leader at the tender age of 22.

"You sit there in the dressing room and you're looking at Miro Heiskanen, you're feeling pretty good about your chances," according to Bowness. "It gives us a big boost of confidence when Miro's in that locker room with everybody."

It's a heavy responsibility but Heiskanen wears it well.

SETH JONES

Blackhawks | Defense | 4

Ronald "Popeye" Jones was a journeyman basketball player, which took him through six NBA cities, including one year in Denver. It was there that his sons fell in love with hockey.

Once 6-year-old Seth saw the Colorado Avalanche in Game 7 of the Stanley Cup Final, he was hooked. "They won the Cup there in 2001 and I was able to go to that game," said Seth. "It was Ray Bourque's first Cup and Sakic passed it to him. That jumped up my love for the game . . . You don't get many chances to go to a Stanley Cup game and that was a special one."

Knowing more about the hardwood, Popeye sought advice from Avalanche captain and fellow Pepsi Center tenant Joe Sakic. "He looked and saw how tall I was,"

recalled Popeye. "Joe wasn't a big guy. He said, 'By the looks of you, they are going to be very tall. Make sure they know how to skate.'"

So Popeye put his sons into figure skating, and as Seth grew into his 6-foot-4, 213-pound frame, he remained a smooth and efficient skater.

If Popeye couldn't impart hockey wisdom on his sons, he could share the lessons he learned through chess. "Control the middle of the ice the way you control the middle of the board and think two or three moves ahead of everyone," advised Popeye.

Seth took to the game quickly, choosing defense because he could see the whole ice and control play strategically. After two years with the U.S. National

Team Development Program, during which he won back-to-back gold medals at the Under-18 World Championship, he played for the Western Hockey League's Portland Winterhawks, where he was named WHL Rookie of the Year in 2012–13. He was the number one ranked skater heading into the 2013 NHL Entry Draft, and most experts assumed the top pick was going to be either Jones or the Halifax Mooseheads' Nathan MacKinnon.

Jones' Team USA won gold at the 2013 World Junior tournament, beating MacKinnon and Canada in the semifinals, but MacKinnon got a small measure of revenge when his Mooseheads beat Jones and the Winterhawks in the 2013 Memorial Cup final.

While a return to Colorado as the first overall selection would have been nice for Jones, the Avalanche took MacKinnon with the top pick. Surprisingly, Jones fell to the Nashville Predators at fourth.

Stuck behind righties Shea Weber and Ryan Ellis on the Nashville depth chart, Jones was traded to the Columbus Blue Jackets, a move he admitted was devastating.

The passion of Columbus fans won him over, and he grew under the tutelage of coach John Tortorella, setting career highs in goals (16), assists (41) and points (57) and finishing fourth in Norris Trophy voting in 2017–18.

Jones played in his third All-Star Game in 2020 but missed the end of the regular season following ankle surgery. With an assist from the pandemic, he was ready for the delayed playoffs, and after upsetting the Toronto Maple Leafs, Columbus faced the Tampa Bay Lightning.

The Lightning were seeking revenge after the President's Trophy winners were swept in the first round by the Blue Jackets in 2019, a postseason in which Jones had nine points in 10 games. The first game of their 2020 series went to quintuple overtime, and Jones set an NHL record by being on the ice for over an hour. After playing 65:06 he said he felt "fine." Tampa won that game and the series in five.

In the midst of a roster teardown in 2021 and knowing he was unlikely to sign long-term, Columbus sent Jones to the Chicago Blackhawks in a blockbuster trade. He then signed an eight-year, $76 million contract extension.

Jones earned his pay in 2021–22, skating 26:13 a game to top the NHL. He also had 51 points, 14th among defensemen and the second highest of his career, including a career-best 46 assists, but the Blackhawks missed the playoffs and no one is harder on themselves than Jones.

"I had some good moments in the year and had some not-so-great moments," assessed Jones. "I obviously have put a lot of pressure on myself to be the best player I can be."

Interim head coach Derek King was won over, however: "He's an elite hockey player. He impressed me a lot. If he were a little more vocal, too, which he's starting to be, I wouldn't doubt seeing him wearing a letter — like, a big letter — down the road, if ever an opportunity comes for him, because he's a class act."

Won gold at the 2011 and 2012 Under-18 World Championship
Won gold at the 2013 World Junior Championship
Named WHL Rookie of the Year in 2013
Played in three NHL All-Star Games (2017, 2019, 2020)

MARC-ANDRE FLEURY

Wild | Goalie | 29

The first pick in the 2003 NHL Entry Draft, after the Pittsburgh Penguins traded up from third, Marc-Andre Fleury was tending goal for Canada at the 2004 World Juniors and showing why he'd been top choice.

A year after being named top goalie at the 2003 World Juniors in Halifax, the native of Sorel, Quebec, and star of the Quebec Major Junior Hockey League's Cape Breton Screaming Eagles was on his way to a repeat. But up 3–1 in the third period of the 2004 gold medal game against the Americans, he let in three goals, including the game-winner — a failed clearing attempt he put in off his own teammate. Team USA's Al Montoya won gold and the goaltending award, but while he became a journeyman, Fleury became a legend.

At his first NHL training camp, Fleury faced Mario Lemieux, one of the greatest players to ever pull on a sweater. He was so star-struck he kept the puck from his first shot. In his first NHL game, against the Los Angeles Kings at the Igloo in Pittsburgh, he allowed a goal on the first shot but then stopped 46 of the next 47. That resiliency would be a hallmark of his career.

There were some lean early years in Pittsburgh, but the Penguins drafted Evgeni Malkin and Sidney Crosby in consecutive years and started building a dynasty. In 2008 they lost to a Detroit Red Wings team stocked with legends in the Stanley Cup Final, but in a rematch one year later Fleury stopped a wide-open Nicklas Lidstrom — Hall of Famer and seven-time Norris Trophy winner — with seconds left in Game 7 to seal the 2009 championship.

When Pittsburgh won the Stanley Cup again in 2016, Matt Murray was the number one goalie. The following year, they split time on the 2017 championship run, but the Penguins decided to stick with a newer model in Murray, who is 10 years younger, and left Fleury unprotected in the expansion draft.

After 13 seasons, 375 wins in the regular season and another 62 in the playoffs, Fleury was available. The grateful Vegas Golden Knights snapped him up, giving them instant legitimacy and leadership.

Motivated and refreshed by the change in 2017–18, Fleury was third in the NHL in goals-against average (2.24) and tied for sixth in save percentage (.927) with Vezina Trophy winner Pekka Rinne.

In the postseason all Fleury did was lead the first-year team to the Stanley Cup Final with a jaw-dropping .947 save percentage, 1.68 goals-against average and four shutouts through the first three rounds. It was his fifth trip to the final and one of the most unlikely playoff runs in NHL history.

In 2020–21, at the age of 36 and in his 17th season, Fleury was 26-10-0 and third in the NHL in wins, shutouts (six), goals-against average (1.98), and save percentage (.928). He started the season 5-0-0 and won each of his final nine starts before taking home his first Vezina Trophy.

Fleury also shared the William Jennings Trophy for fewest goals against with Robin Lehner. It was their final act together; the success of the Golden Knights meant making hard salary cap decisions, and they traded the older Fleury and his $7 million salary to the Chicago Blackhawks in the offseason.

Taken off guard and concerned about the upheaval for his wife, Veronique, and children, Estelle, Scarlett and James, one of whom lives with anxiety, Fleury contemplated retirement but ultimately reported to Chicago.

The Blackhawks underachieved, and with Fleury's contract about to expire he was acquired by former Pittsburgh teammate and current Minnesota Wild general manager Bill Guerin at the trade deadline. He went 9-2-0 with the Wild and played the first five games of a six game first round loss to the St. Louis Blues, tying Grant Fuhr for third all-time in playoff wins with 92 in the process.

Fleury sits alone in third in regular season wins, behind only Martin Brodeur and just 31 back of Patrick Roy. All three hail from Quebec, and they're the two reasons he became a goalie in the first place. Fleury also joined them as the only three with 500 wins, a milestone he reached in style just down the river from home with a shutout against the Canadiens in Montreal on Dec. 9, 2021.

Entering free agency for the very first time, the universally respected and beloved goalie chose to stay in Minnesota. His next stop will be Toronto, with his plaque up in the Hall of Fame.

- Won silver at the 2003 and 2004 World Junior Championship
- Won three Stanley Cups (2009, 2016, 2017)
- Won gold at the 2010 Winter Olympics
- Named to five NHL All-Star Games (2011, 2015, 2018, 2019, 2020)
- Won the Vezina and William Jennings Trophies in 2021
- First among active goalies and third all-time in wins (520) at the end of the 2021–22 season

FILIP FORSBERG

Predators | Left Wing | 9

Filip Forsberg's memories of his father, Patrik, playing professional hockey in Sweden and Norway are a little hazy. After Patrik retired in 2002, he coached Filip and his younger brother, Fredrik, in Ostervala, a town of less than 2,000 people in eastern Sweden, with one overriding lesson. "To this day, it's just to work hard. I think that's the biggest thing. He tells me all the time that he wishes he would have worked harder," says Filip.

Message received. Fredrik was the leading scorer for HV71 in the Swedish Hockey League in 2021–22, while Filip set two major records for the Nashville Predators.

Filip was originally drafted by the Washington Capitals 11th overall in 2012. Central Scouting had him rated fourth in the draft class, but he slipped, in part because he had just one point at the 2012 World Junior Championship, even as Sweden won gold.

Forsberg signed an entry-level contract but never donned a Capitals sweater. He was traded to the Nashville Predators for veteran Martin Erat and prospect Michael Latta at the 2013 trade deadline.

After Forsberg's 2012–13 season in Sweden ended with 33 points in 38 games and his Leksands earned promotion to the top division, the Predators brought him Stateside for his first taste of NHL hockey. He spent most of the following season with the Milwaukee Admirals of the American Hockey League, while redeeming himself at his third World Juniors. He had eight assists and 12 points in seven games, was named the tournament's Most Valuable Player, and won his second silver in a row.

By 2014–15 Forsberg proved he could play at the highest levels. He had 26 goals and 63 points in a full NHL season, setting the Predators' rookie record, added six points in six playoff games, and then went to the World Championship and scored eight goals in eight games.

After playing every game during his first three full seasons in Nashville, Forsberg ran into a string of injury troubles, missing a combined 56 games over the next four seasons. An upper body injury cost him nine games early in the 2021–22 season, but it turned out to be a banner year.

On March 19, 2022, Forsberg scored his 211th goal in a win over the Toronto Maple Leafs to break David Legwand's franchise record for regular-season career goals scored. Legwand took 956 games to set it, Forsberg took 546 games to break it.

Two days later Forsberg had two goals and three assists to help beat the Anaheim Ducks. With his 35th goal, he broke the Predators' record for goals in a season, passing Viktor Arvidsson's mark from 2018–19.

"We couldn't let him keep it for too long when he's not on our team anymore," joked Forsberg.

Forsberg finished 2021–22 with 42 goals, tied for ninth in the NHL, and in 69 games he also set career highs with 42 assists and 84 points.

At the end of the 2021–22 season, his all-time Predators record in regular season goals was 220, and he was also holding the franchise record for playoff goals (28) and playoff points (53). When Nashville made the Stanley Cup Final in 2017, losing to the Pittsburgh Penguins in six games, Forsberg led them with nine goals and 16 points. A year later he led the Predators in playoff scoring again with seven goals and another 16 points in only 13 games, including the goal of the playoffs in Game 1 of the first round against the Colorado Avalanche.

"He thinks of doing things out there that wouldn't even happen in my dreams," said teammate Austin Watson afterward.

Forsberg's contract expired in 2022, and as as one NHL executive put it succinctly: "Pay him or rebuild."

The Predators chose the former, signing the 27-year-old franchise icon to an eight-year, $68 million contract extension so he can add to the record book and the young fan base in Tennessee.

"Every little kid here in Nashville probably runs around on the street with their hockey stick when they score calling themselves Forsberg," says teammate Ryan Johansen.

Won gold at the 2012 World Junior Championship

Won silver at the 2013 and 2014 World Junior Championship and named Most Valuable Player in 2014

NHL All-Rookie Team in 2014–15

Played in the 2015 NHL All-Star Game

Won gold at the 2018 World Championship

Predators franchise leader in career goals (220 at end of 2021–22 season)

VLADIMIR TARASENKO

Blues | Right Wing | 91

Vladimir Tarasenko scored on the first two shots of his NHL career. The goals came on January 19, 2013, against the Detroit Red Wings, the former team of his idol Sergei Fedorov and one of the reasons Tarasenko wears No. 91. It's also the year of his birth, in Novosibirsk, Siberia.

Tarasenko spent much of his youth there being raised by his grandfather and namesake while his father, Andrei, was pursuing his own hockey dreams.

The elder Vladimir was the director of a soccer academy, but his grandson wanted to follow in his father's skates. The young man was groomed to succeed with a little tough love. "When [Vladimir] had a fever my wife would still dress him warmly and take him for a walk outside in winter," recalled his grandfather fondly.

Tarasenko made HC Sibir Novosibirsk's second team when he was 14, scoring seven goals in one game that season. The next pre-season he earned a tryout with the first team, which was coached by his father.

If there were any questions of nepotism, Tarasenko answered them by scoring a goal the first time he touched the puck in the Kontinental Hockey League.

But it wasn't always smooth sailing for father and son. "They were always punching each other, screaming at each other," said Jori Lehtera, Tarasenko's ex-teammate with the St. Louis Blues and Novosibirsk. "They had more like a coach-player relationship."

Tarasenko eventually left his hometown to play for SKA St. Petersburg, where he was named captain at the age of 18. After he represented Russia at the 2010 World Junior Championship, the Blues traded David Rundblad to Ottawa to draft him 16th overall.

In 2011 Tarasenko returned to the World Juniors as Team Russia's captain. He left the gold medal game with a rib injury in the second period but came back for the third when Russia trailed Canada 3-0. The captain spearheaded the comeback with the game-tying goal and an assist on the go-ahead goal in a 5-3 win.

By 2014–15 Tarasenko had established himself as an NHL star. He led the Blues with 37 goals, the start of five straight seasons of at least 33. He was third in the NHL in that span with 182 goals, trailing leader Alex Ovechkin and just one goal behind John Tavares.

In 2015 the Blues rewarded Tarasenko with an eight-year contract averaging $7.5 million per season, the highest in franchise history. In 2015–16 he led the Blues in regular-season (40) and playoff goals (nine) as they reached the Western Conference Final.

Tarasenko also met Arianna Dougan, who was fighting neuroblastoma, at the Blues' Hockey Fights Cancer event in 2015. In 2017 he brought her on the Blues charter plane to Arizona and Colorado for her 11th

birthday. Arianna died later that year, but her memory was alive and inspirational in 2019. Tarasenko was coming back from reconstructive shoulder surgery in the off-season, and the Blues were last overall on January 3. But the team rose up the standings in the second half and stormed through the playoffs, in large part because of Tarasenko's improved play at both ends of the rink.

Tarasenko contributed 11 goals and had an eight-game point streak in the playoffs as the Blues beat the Boston Bruins in seven games to capture the first Stanley Cup in franchise history.

The night the Blues advanced to the Final, he sent a text to Lori Zucker, Arianna's mom. It simply said, "She is in my heart."

The next two years were tougher for Tarasenko than most. He was limited to just 34 games with more shoulder problems, and he and the Blues were on again, off again with their affection for each other. Tarasenko reportedly requested a trade, while the Blues left him unprotected in the 2021 expansion draft.

Won gold at the 2011 World Junior Championship	
Played in three NHL All-Star Games (2015, 2016, 2017)	
Featured on the cover of EA Sports' NHL 17	
Won the Stanley Cup in 2019	

But Tarasenko was resurgent in 2021–22, playing 75 games, scoring 34 goals and having career-highs in both assists (48) and points (82). He added six goals in the playoffs, including the two fastest goals in team playoff history and a natural hat trick in a win over the Minnesota Wild, before the Blues lost to the juggernaut Colorado Avalanche in round two.

Early in the season, his shoulder had healed and the rift appeared to be too, at least with the fans, who chanted his name after two goals and a win. "That was a special moment," said Tarasenko. "It was very emotional. We always have support from the real fans. I always said it in the interviews: Our family got so much help from people from St. Louis."

MATS ZUCCARELLO

Wild | Right Wing | 36

seen it 1,500 times. I know every bit of it by heart — and I'm sure she does too."

Zuccarello skated on frozen ponds in the winter and in the summer he'd play handball, soccer and floorball. "The kick-pass is an underrated skill," he says. "A lot of battles along the boards are won with crafty feet — don't forget that."

The unusual route to the NHL first went through the Frisk Asker program in Norway, where Zuccarello had 34 goals and 59 points in 43 games as a 19-year-old in 2006–07, followed by a 64-point season and 12 goals and 27 points in 15 playoff games.

That got Zuccarello into the upper echelon of European hockey with the legendary MoDo of the Swedish Hockey League. In his first season, he had 40 points in 35 games, and in 2009–10 he led the league in scoring with 64 points and won the Golden Helmet as league MVP.

But it was on hockey's biggest stage that Zuccarello finally caught the eye of NHL brass. Norway finished 10th at the 2010 Vancouver Olympics, but he stood out among the world's best. He signed as a free agent with the New York Rangers in May 2010 and made his NHL debut that December, after an eye-opening introduction.

"My first camp with the Rangers I thought, I'm not good enough. What am I doing here? I'd see Marian Gaborik skating circles around All-Star defensemen and think, Look at that guy. I'm not even close to that," Zuccarello wrote.

Time in the American Hockey League honed Zuccarello's North American game, and playing under NHL coach Paul Maurice for Metallurg Magnitogorsk in the KHL during the 2012 NHL lockout also bolstered his confidence.

It coalesced for Zuccarello in 2013–14. He led the Rangers in scoring with 59 points in 77 games and added five goals and 13 points in 25 playoff

I n the long history of short, undrafted Norwegians in the NHL, Mats Zuccarello might be the best. The 5-foot-8 winger grew up in Loren, a suburb of Oslo, where hockey wasn't nearly as popular as in neighboring Sweden. He'd get 30 minutes a week of NHL highlights, so when he found a VHS copy of the Colorado Avalanche's 2001 Stanley Cup championship on a trip across the border, he knew he had to have it.

"To kids growing up in North America, finding it wouldn't be such a big deal. But to me, it was like striking gold," wrote Zuccarello in The Players' Tribune. "45 glorious minutes of uninterrupted hockey perfection. I begged my mom, 'Please, please, please! Can we get it?' She bought it for me. I've probably

games, while becoming the first Norwegian to play in the Stanley Cup Final, a five-game loss to the Los Angeles Kings.

A fan favorite and three-time winner of the Rangers' Steven McDonald Extra Effort Award, Zuccarello averaged 56 points a season from 2013–14 through 2017–18, although his career nearly came to an end in the 2015 playoffs. He took a slapshot to the head, suffering a fractured skull and brain contusion that left him in the hospital for three days, unable to speak or move his arm.

After physical and speech therapy, Zuccarello's return to the ice was inspirational. He played 81 games in 2015–16 and had career highs of 26 goals and 61

Named Norwegian Player of the Year seven times

Won the Guldhjälmen (Golden Helmet) as Swedish Hockey League MVP in 2010

Represented Norway at the 2010 and 2014 Olympic Games

Won silver with Team Europe at the 2016 World Cup of Hockey

Finalist for the 2016 Bill Masterton Trophy

points to lead the Rangers and earn a nomination for the Bill Masterton Trophy.

In 2019, with the Rangers in rebuild mode, Zuccarello was sent to the Dallas Stars as the trade deadline approached. A broken arm cost him most of the regular season but he returned for the playoffs with 11 points in 13 games. The unrestricted free agent then signed a five-year contract with the Minnesota Wild on July 1, 2019.

Zuccarello has carved out a long and productive career, but at 34 he exploded, setting career-highs in assists (55) and points (79) in 70 games played in 2021–22. The season included a ten-game point streak and team record six-game multipoint streak, the last of which came after the Rangers retired the number of Zuccarello's good friend and former teammate, Swedish goalie Henrik Lundqvist. The cheers at Madison Square Garden that night were almost as loud for the Norwegian.

"You've been here for nine years, and they were great to me when I was here. Still are," said Zuccarello. "But I'm in a great place right now (in) Minnesota. Love everything about it, how we play as a team and the fans there. So I've got the best of both worlds, for sure."

Worlds apart from Loren and the NHL on a VCR.

SHAYNE GOSTISBEHERE

Coyotes | Defense | 14

Say what you will about commissioner Gary Bettman's Great Southern Experiment, but it is starting to produce high-end talent from some unlikely places.

Shayne Gostisbehere was born in Pembroke Pines, Florida, in 1993, the same year the Florida Panthers came into the NHL. His father, Regis, had moved there from France to play jai alai, and he met his French-Canadian bride-to-be, Christine, working at a jai alai court.

Shayne's sister took figure skating lessons at the Panthers' training facility, and he would tag along. He eventually stuck around the rink as a member of the Junior Panthers. His dad knew little about the game, so his grandfather, Denis, helped out. "I bought him a helmet, got him into a league and coached him for

years before [former Panther] Ray Sheppard took over," said Denis. "He was always the smallest kid on the team, but I told him there are two things he has to remember: 'Let your stick and skates do the talking and no one will turn you down.'"

With his grandfather's wise words in mind, Gostisbehere left Florida to play hockey at South Kent School in Connecticut for his final two years of high school. He had 36 points in 24 games as a senior but went undrafted in 2011. Philadelphia took a flyer on Ghost in the 2012 draft, choosing him in the third round, 78th overall, after his first season at Union College in Schenectady, New York.

Gostisbehere won a gold medal with Team USA at the 2013 World Juniors, and in 2014 he was named Frozen Four MVP as Union won its first national championship. In the title game at Philadelphia's Wells Fargo Center, he had a goal and two assists and was plus-7 in a 7–4 win over the University of Minnesota.

Flyers fans would have to wait for him to light up the rink again, however. After five games with the Lehigh Valley Phantoms of the American Hockey League, Gostisbehere tore his ACL and was lost for a year. He started the 2015–16 season with the Phantoms and finished it with the Flyers, coming second in Calder Trophy voting, ahead of Connor McDavid. "It definitely caught me by surprise," said Gostisbehere.

Still undersized, Gostisbehere used his speed and creativity to score 17 goals and 46 points, 18 of which came during a 15-game point streak, the longest by a rookie defenseman in NHL history and matching the longest by any defenseman since Chris Chelios in 1995. The last point of the streak was an overtime winner, which made him the first rookie in history to score four overtime goals in a season.

Gostisbehere was named to the All-Rookie Team and selected for the 23-and-under Team North America squad at the 2016 World Cup of Hockey, where he

had four assists to tie for the team lead in points.

In his second season, however, Gostisbehere came back down to earth. The rookie phenom ended up watching games from the press box as a healthy scratch before picking up his play late in the season.

It's become the theme of Gostisbehere's career. After 65 points in 2017–18, which was fourth among all defensemen, just two points behind second and two ahead of Norris Trophy winner Victor Hedman, to go along with elite possession metrics, he crashed back to earth with 37 points in 2018–19.

A healthy scratch and a trade request in 2019–20, knee surgery in 2020, and time on the taxi squad in 2021 were the last plunge on the Philadelphia roller-coaster for Gostisbehere. Retooling, the Flyers decided to move forward without his salary cap hit and traded him to the Arizona Coyotes. He left the team fourth among defensemen in franchise history in goals (60), sixth in assists (159) and fifth in points (219).

Only 28, the change of scenery worked and

Won gold at the 2013 World Junior Championship	
Won the NCAA championship and named Frozen Four MVP in 2014	
Set the NHL record for longest point streak by a rookie defenseman (15 games)	
Holds the NHL rookie record with four overtime goals in a season	

Gostisbehere rose like a phoenix in Arizona. He had his second-best season in 2021–22 in goals (14), assists (37) and points (51), and the power play quarterback had a point on 84 percent of the goals he was on the ice for with the man advantage, tops in the NHL.

"From the moment the puck was dropped in training camp, Shayne was one of the first guys to kind of buy in to what we were trying to do. He had some bite," said Coyotes general manager Bill Armstrong, who's been a fan since Gostisbehere was at Union.

"You could tell he was playing to make a difference. He was all in, and he's been great right from there."

DEVON TOEWS

Avalanche | Defense | 7

Devon Toews has a history of being overlooked. The product of the Abbotsford Minor Hockey Association made a name for himself in the British Columbia Hockey League with 29 points in 54 games as a rookie for the Surrey Eagles, and then 47 points in 48 games in his second season as his team won the 2013 BCHL title.

"When he was in Surrey we knew he was going to be able to be a pro," said his father, Werner. "He had a special skill set. Anyone that coached him or ex-pros that knew him just told us that he's got the skill set — he'll go pro."

But his son wasn't even chosen in the Western Hockey League draft, so he accepted a scholarship at Quinnipiac University in Connecticut instead.

Matt Erhart, the head coach of the Eagles at the time and former Quinnipiac Bobcat, had tipped off the school. "He said he's a little scrawny but he has a really high hockey IQ and he'd be a good fit for how Quinnipiac plays," said coach Rand Pecknold. "We started watching him more as he played with Surrey and we just loved everything he did. You can't teach hockey IQ and he had such a great feel for the game."

Toews had already been passed over in the NHL draft twice, but after getting 17 points in 37 games as a freshman, the New York Islanders picked him in the fourth round, 108th overall, in 2014. He then had 20 points as a sophomore in 2014–15, and as he grew and got stronger, he put up 30 points in 40 games and Quinnipiac won an Eastern College Athletic

Conference title in 2015–16.

Toews spent the next two seasons in the American Hockey League with the Bridgeport Sound Tigers. He had 45 points in 76 games in 2016–17 and was named to the AHL All-Rookie Team. He also won the fastest skater competition at the 2017 AHL All-Star Game with a time of 13.478 seconds, almost a dead heat with Connor McDavid's winning time of 13.310 at the NHL version that year.

After recording 86 points in 130 games with Bridgeport from 2016–18, Toews was called up by the Islanders in December 2018 and got his first NHL point on January 3, 2019, when he scored the overtime winner against the Chicago Blackhawks. He had 18 points in 48 games that season and improved to 28 points in 68 games in 2019–20, adding 10 points in 22 playoff games to help the Islanders reach the 2020 Eastern Conference Final.

Settling into a regular NHL role, Toews was two days into married life in October 2020 when he was traded to the Colorado Avalanche for two second round draft picks. He then signed a four-year, $16.4 million contract that's starting to look like the biggest bargain in the NHL.

In 2020–21, Toews led the Avalanche in average ice-time (24:46) and was tied for second in the NHL and first among defensemen with a plus-29.

Toews was limited to 66 games in 2021–22 because of shoulder surgery, but he had 57 points, tied for ninth in scoring among defensemen. He was fifth in even-strength points with 45, and all four ahead of him were Norris Trophy winners or finalists. He was also ninth in average ice time (25:22), and first among defensemen and fourth in the NHL with a plus-52.

With Toews in the lineup, the Avalanche were 51-9-5, and without him they were 5-10-1. When the playoffs came, he contributed 13 points and a plus-8 in the first 15 games, and finished with 15 points in 20 games while playing 25:53 a night for the Stanley Cup champions.

Partnered with Cale Makar, they were discussed as a ready-made pair for Team Canada's blue line in Beijing before the NHL pulled out of the Olympics. Makar won the 2022 Norris and Conn Smythe Trophies, and as he became one of the NHL's biggest stars Toews was relegated to the background, which is "unfortunate," according to Makar.

"He's one of the best defensemen in the league," said Makar of his partner. "And obviously he's a guy that might be a little bit undervalued, but he's such an important player for us. He is a driving force for us on the back end. So calm. And his presence is just so felt every time he's on the ice."

But Toews is fine with being overshadowed. "I hate the cameras, honestly," he said. But as half of the best defensive pair in the NHL and with a shiny new Stanley Cup ring on his finger, it's going to be pretty hard to avoid the spotlight.

Played in the 2017 AHL All-Star Game and won fastest skater

Named to the AHL All-Rookie Team in 2016–17

First among NHL defensemen in plus-minus in 2020–21 (+29) and 2021–22 (+52)

2022 Stanley Cup champion

DARCY KUEMPER

Avalanche | Goalie | 35

Goaltender is the most important position in hockey but the hardest to scout. Most are picked outside the first round and take years to develop into NHL starters. Darcy Kuemper is no exception. His path started with an ideal slice of Canadiana on the outdoor rink a few minutes from his home, with his mother ready to thaw his feet, or playing ball hockey at every opportunity with some of the same friends he still spends his summers fishing with on Saskatchewan lakes.

When Kuemper joined the local hockey program, he rotated through the goalie position with all his teammates. Like many a young player, he was drawn to the cool pads and playing an entire game, unlike many he grew to be 6-foot-5 and flexible.

After he got his own set when he was 12, Kuemper was either going to be an NHL goalie or a police officer, like his father. Chosen in the sixth round of the 2009 NHL draft, 160th overall, by the Minnesota Wild, the only thin blue line in his future would be the one his defensemen patrolled.

Kuemper spent two years in the Western Hockey League with the Red Deer Rebels after being drafted, and in the 2010–11 season, he posted a 45-12-3-2 record, leading all WHL goaltenders in wins, goals-against average (1.86) and save percentage (.933), and tying a WHL record with 13 shutouts. He was named the WHL's Top Goaltender and league MVP, as well as the CHL Goaltender of the Year.

Following two seasons spent between the East Coast Hockey League and the American Hockey League, Kuemper made his NHL debut in February 2013, and the following season he spent time with the Iowa Wild in the AHL during the lockout.

Backing up Ilya Bryzgalov to start the 2014 NHL playoffs, Kuemper was called upon after the Wild went down two games to none to the Colorado Avalanche in the first round. He started Game 3 and earned the first playoff shutout in franchise history, then won two more games before injuring his leg in Minnesota's Game 7 win, sidelining him for the rest of the playoffs.

Kuemper started strong in the 2014–15 season with shutouts in three of his first four games but lost the starting job to Devan Dubnyk. In 2015–16 he set a Wild record by earning at least a point in each of his first eight games but didn't get consistent starts and struggled with motivation.

A free agent after the 2016–17 season, Kuemper signed a one-year contract with the Los Angeles Kings, and under the tutelage of goalie coach Bill Ranford, a Stanley Cup and Conn Smythe winner with the Edmonton Oilers, he was rejuvenated. Kuemper went 10-1-3 with a 2.10 goals-against average and .932 save

percentage in 19 games with the Kings before being acquired by the Arizona Coyotes at the 2018 trade deadline.

Kuemper fulfilled his potential as the starter with his first full NHL workload in 2018–19. He went 27-20-8 with a 2.33 GAA and .925 save percentage, and set career highs with 55 games played, including 21 straight starts, and five shutouts. From January 6 onwards, he posted a 22-9-5 record and a .933 save percentage.

In 2019–20 Kuemper was third in the NHL with a .928 save percentage and his 2.22 goals-against average was fourth. He was named to the All-Star Game and finished seventh in Vezina voting despite playing only 29 games.

At the end of the 2020–21 season, Kuemper traveled to Latvia and led Canada to gold at the World Championship, and a month later he was traded to the Avalanche, who were looking for the final piece for a team loaded with talent. He didn't disappoint.

Kuemper was 37-12-4, tied for fourth in the NHL in wins, fifth in save percentage (.921), and 11th in goals-against average (2.54) in 2021–22. In the playoffs he had a .934 save percentage in the first round against the Nashville Predators until he took the blade of a stick through his facemask in Game 3. He returned to face the St. Louis Blues in round two but had to leave Game 1 of the Western Conference Final against the Edmonton Oilers with his vision still impaired.

Kuemper was back for the Stanley Cup Final and started every game. He was pulled in Game 3 but outdueled reigning Conn Smythe winner Andrei Vasilevskiy at the other end and held the two-time defending champion Tampa Bay Lightning to one goal in Game 6 as the Avalanche won their first title since 2001.

"It's the hardest thing I've ever done but every second's been worth it," said Kuemper on the ice after hoisting the Stanley Cup.

"My family never let me stop believing."

PACIFIC DIVISION

FIRST TEAM

SECOND TEAM

TAXI SQUAD

The following season Draisaitl scored seven goals and 10 assists in his first 10 NHL games, which made him the first Oiler to start a season with 17 points in 10 games since Messier in 1989–90.

Draisaitl finished the 2015–16 season with 19 goals and 51 points in 72 games, and though the Oilers missed the playoffs for the 10th straight season, they had the new Messier to their young Gretzky.

Connor McDavid, the first overall pick in 2015 who became the captain in 2016, is the man in Edmonton. Draisaitl is the wingman, in a literal sense. Draisaitl plays on McDavid's right side when he's not center-ing the second line. And it's become the best one-two punch in the NHL.

The 2016–17 season was a rebirth for the franchise. Playing in a new arena, the Oilers tied for seventh overall in the NHL, and Draisaitl finished eighth in the league with 77 points, on 29 goals and 48 assists. They also had their first taste of playoff success.

After dispatching the San Jose Sharks in the first round, the Oilers faced the Anaheim Ducks in the Western Conference semifinals. In Game 6 Draisaitl had the first playoff hat trick by an Oiler since 2000 and added two assists in the 7–1 win, putting him second in playoff scoring with 16 points.

The Oilers lost in seven, then missed the playoffs in the two years following despite the high-scoring exploits of their two leaders.

Draisaitl had 25 goals in 2017–18 and then doubled that in 2018–19, reaching the 50-goal plateau after a stretch of 17 goals in 18 games in the second half of the season and three goals in the final two games. He finished just one behind Alex Ovechkin for the Maurice Richard Trophy, and it was the first time an Oiler had 50 goals since Gretzky and Jari Kurri each hit the mark in 1986–87. He was also the first player since 2011–12 to have at least 50 goals and 100 points in a season, finishing with 105. A year later he upped the ante again.

H e was called the German Gretzky before he'd ever suited up for Edmonton, but when Leon Draisaitl did pull on the Oilers jersey, he made like Mark Messier.

Edmonton drafted Draisaitl third overall in 2014, and in his first 37 NHL games, in 2014–15, Draisaitl had just two goals and seven assists, so the Oilers sent him down to the Kelowna Rockets. Back in the West-ern Hockey League, he was named playoff MVP after his 28 points in 19 postseason games sent Kelowna to the Memorial Cup, where he led the tournament in scoring and won tournament MVP despite losing the championship game to the Oshawa Generals.

Named WHL playoff MVP in 2015

Named MVP at the 2015 Memorial Cup

Won the Art Ross Trophy, Ted Lindsay Award and Hart Trophy in 2019–2020

Led the NHL in game-winning goals twice (2019–20, 2021–22)

Played in three NHL All-Star Games (2019, 2020, 2022)

NHL's active leader in shooting percentage (17.6)

The 2019–20 season was memorable for a lot of the wrong reasons, including an early playoff exit for the Oilers in the Edmonton bubble, but for Draisaitl it was the regular season of a lifetime. He led the NHL with 67 assists and 110 points, 13 ahead of second place McDavid, to win the Art Ross Trophy. He also took home the Hart Trophy and Ted Lindsay Award to sweep the MVP awards, the latter announced by Messier.

Draisaitl switched back with his teammate in the abbreviated 2020–21 season, finishing second in the NHL and to McDavid in assists (53) and points (84), and he handed the Hart across the dressing room. But once again regular season accolades didn't precede postseason success, and the Oilers were out in round

one of the North Division playoffs.

In 2021–22, Draisaitl almost had both. He set a new career high in goals with 55, good for second in the NHL, and he tied his MVP season with 110 points, which was fourth in the league.

In the playoffs the Oilers exorcised some demons with a first-round victory over the Los Angeles Kings in seven games and a wild Battle of Alberta win over the Calgary Flames in five. It only ended when they ran into the juggernaut Colorado Avalanche, and it wasn't the fault of the stars.

When they were eliminated, McDavid and Draisaitl sat first and second in playoff scoring with 33 and 32 points, respectively. Draisaitl had an incredible 25 assists in 16 games to lead the NHL, including four in the last game against Colorado and four twice against Calgary. He's only the second player after Gretzky with 25 assists in 16 playoff games or less, and with seven three-point games in one postseason. And he did it all on one leg.

Playing on a severely sprained ankle suffered in round one, he displayed a Messier-like will to win. At this point though, it's enough to say he played exactly like Draisaitl.

Johnny Hockey's nickname began as a play on Johnny Football's. It invokes the youthful exuberance that both Johnnys displayed while tearing up the collegiate ranks in their respective sports. While Texas A&M quarterback Johnny Manziel burned out quickly, Johnny Gaudreau is now among the best in the business.

The native of Salem, New Jersey, was a child prodigy, skating rings around older kids. When Jane Gaudreau suggested to her husband, Guy, that Johnny might be in the NHL some day, Guy tempered expectations: "Whoa, you sound like some of my crazy hockey parents. He's not going to the NHL."

Guy wasn't uninformed. A member of the athletic hall of fame at Norwich University in Vermont, he was hockey director at Hollydell Ice Arena, where Johnny learned to skate.

Still dominating while at Gloucester Catholic High School, Gaudreau joined the Dubuque Fighting Saints of the United States Hockey League in 2010–11. The 17-year-old scored 72 points in 60 games and earned Rookie of the Year honors.

That convinced the Calgary Flames to draft Gaudreau in the fourth round in 2011, 104th overall, well ahead of Central Scouting's projection of 193rd overall. With Gaudreau clocking in at 5-foot-6 and 137 pounds, even that projection was generous for a winger of his size.

Gaudreau chose to hone his game (and grow) at Boston College, winning the NCAA title in his freshman year after being cut from USA Hockey's 2012

World Junior team. "He takes those setbacks, uses them to motivate him more and it has furthered his determination," said former Boston College associate head coach Greg Brown of the snub. Gaudreau made the World Junior team in 2013 and led the tournament with seven goals en route to the U.S. winning gold.

A Hobey Baker finalist for NCAA player of the year as a sophomore, Gaudreau stuck around Boston College to play another year with younger brother Matt in 2013–14. He won the award as a junior and the next day signed with Calgary. The Flames welcomed him in style, flying him out by private jet to their last game of the 2013–14 season. After munching on Skittles during the flight, he repaid them with a goal on his first NHL shot.

In his first full season, Gaudreau was a finalist for the Calder Trophy after scoring 24 goals, leading all rookies in assists with 40 and tying for the rookie lead in points with 64. He also helped Calgary reach the playoffs for the first time in six years and led the team with nine points in 11 games. Gaudreau followed that up with 30 goals and 78 points in 2015–16, good for sixth in league scoring.

In 2018–19 Gaudreau had career highs in goals (36), assists (63) and points (99), tying him for seventh in the NHL in points and ninth in assists, and he finished fourth in Hart Trophy voting. A career-defining season topped each of those in 2021–22.

Gaudreau had 40 goals, was third in the league with 75 assists, and his 115 points were tied for second and the most by a Calgary player since Kent Nillson in 1980–81. It was only the 12th time a player has reached at least 110 points since 2007–08, and his plus-64 led the NHL and set a Flames franchise record. He also scored one of the most iconic goals in team history with the overtime winner in Game 7 against

the Dallas Stars in the first round, one of his 14 points in 12 playoff games.

It was a shock when Gaudreau wasn't a Hart Trophy finalist. His 90 points at even strength were 12 ahead of Connor McDavid and 13 more than Auston Matthews, the next two on the list and the two skaters nominated for the Hart. He's also become the Flames' best checker, all 5-foot-9, 165 pounds of him, according to defense-first coach Darryl Sutter.

Gaudreau's career numbers — he's third in the NHL in assists (399), sixth in points (608) and averaging more than a point a game since his first full season — are more than even his mother could've imagined, and now his paycheck might be too.

An unrestricted free agent after being eliminated by the blood rival Edmonton Oilers, Gaudreau left an extra year and millions on the table from Calgary to sign a seven-year, $68.25 million contract with the Columbus Blue Jackets.

In a farewell article, Johnny Ohio wrote about being closer to family and insisted he considered the Flames until the 11th hour before making a decision that vexed Calgary and perplexed the rest of the NHL.

"Maybe that seems messy but life is messy, you know?"

Won gold at the 2013 World Junior Championship

Won the Hobey Baker Award in 2014

Played in six NHL All-Star Games (2015, 2016, 2017, 2018, 2019, 2022)

Named to the NHL All-Rookie Team in 2015

Won the Lady Byng Trophy in 2017

First in the NHL in plus-minus (+64) and tied for second in points (115) in 2021–22

CONNOR McDAVID

Oilers | Center | 97

I n 2015 Edmonton officially stopped calling itself the City of Champions. Posted on signs entering the city, the slogan celebrated the community's response to a 1987 tornado and the hockey team that was in the midst of winning five Stanley Cups. City councillors might have been premature in voting to remove the signs, however. In 2015 the Oilers drafted the most hyped player since Sidney Crosby.

Growing up in Newmarket, Ontario, Connor McDavid always played with older kids, and his York Simcoe Express team won provincial championships in novice, minor atom, atom, minor peewee and peewee. He left to attend what's now known as Blyth Academy,

a school for elite athletes in Toronto. There he proved he didn't have just hockey intellect; he also moved up a year academically.

At 15 McDavid became the third player ever to be granted exceptional player status to join the Ontario Hockey League a year early. The Erie Otters took him first overall, and McDavid won back-to-back OHL and Canadian Hockey League Scholastic Player of the Year awards in 2014 and 2015.

In 2014–15 McDavid won both the OHL and CHL Player of the Year honors, despite missing six weeks with a broken hand. The injury caused a national crisis when it appeared he might not play in the World Juniors, but his cast came off days before it started and he had a tournament-leading eight assists in seven games as Canada won the gold.

McDavid finished the OHL season with 44 goals, 120 points and a plus-60 rating in only 47 games, and he added 49 points in 20 playoff games as the Otters lost to the Oshawa Generals in the final.

Crosby was McDavid's idol, and once McDavid hit the NHL, he proved he was Crosby's heir apparent and equal. Crosby admits the 6-foot-1, 193-pound center is "far and away the fastest guy I've seen," which was proven when McDavid broke the 21-year-old record for fastest skater at the 2017 All-Star Skills Competition, and then won it twice more.

His breathtaking speed is one of the reasons McDavid missed 37 games in his rookie season of 2015–16. He flew full speed into the end boards and broke his collarbone, but he still finished third in Calder Trophy voting after getting 48 points in 45 games.

Prior to the 2016–17 season, the Oilers named McDavid captain at 19 years, 266 days old, making him the youngest captain in NHL history. As the Second Coming of Wayne Gretzky, McDavid led the league with 70 assists and won the Art Ross Trophy with an even 100 points in his second season. At just 20 he also won the Hart Trophy and Ted Lindsay

Award, and for the first time in a decade the Oilers were back in the playoffs.

It was a short-lived resurgence, however. Despite McDavid winning the Ted Lindsay Award and Art Ross again in 2017–18, with 41 goals and 108 points, the Oilers missed the playoffs.

All McDavid has done since then is record 116 points for second in the NHL in 2018–19; 97 points in just 64 games when COVID ended the 2019–20 season early, second in the league again; 105 points in 56 games of the second pandemic-affected season of 2020–21 to win another Art Ross, Ted Lindsay Award and Hart Trophy, unanimously; and career-bests in goals (44), assists (79) and points (123) in 2021–22 to lead the NHL yet again.

They're video game stats, and so are some of his highlights. The best players make the game look easy, and McDavid does that. He can also appear superhuman. He'll score a one-on-four goal in a regular season game that could be the highlight of the season, until he does it again a few weeks later. His turns and stickhandling defy physics and belief, he makes All-Star defensemen look like beer leaguers, and jaded commentators struggle to find comparisons and superlatives.

Won gold at the 2015 World Junior Championship

Won gold at the 2016 World Championship

Won two Hart Trophies (2017, 2021)

Won three Ted Lindsay Awards (2017, 2018, 2021)

Won four Art Ross Trophies (2017, 2018, 2021, 2022)

Played in five NHL All-Star Games (2017, 2018, 2019, 2020, 2022)

But McDavid will be the first to tell you that none of that matters without playoff success, and the Oilers repeatedly fell short in the postseason until 2022. He took his game to a level rarely seen, willing his team to a first-round win over the Los Angeles Kings and taking the heart out of the higher-seeded and hated Calgary Flames before falling to the Colorado Avalanche in the Western Conference Final. He left the playoffs first in scoring with a ridiculous 33 points in 16 games — only Gretzky and Mario Lemieux had playoffs with a higher points-per-game average.

Over a few weeks in the spring McDavid went from the best player of his generation to the conversation about the greatest ever. It'll take a Stanley Cup to get there but Edmonton has a force of nature, with the heart of a champion.

Quintin Hughes was born to play hockey, if not born in a hockey hotbed.

His mother, Ellen, played soccer, lacrosse and hockey at the University of New Hampshire and represented Team USA at the second Women's World Hockey Championship in 1992. She's the one who taught her three sons to skate.

His father, Jim, was a defenseman and captain at Providence College before embarking on a coaching career that took him to the International Hockey League's Orlando Solar Bears, where Quinn was born. From there the family started heading north to more hockey-friendly climates.

When Quinn was two, Jim took an assistant coaching job with the Boston Bruins. Five years later they

packed up for Toronto, where Jim worked for the American Hockey League's Marlies before becoming director of player development for the Maple Leafs. By now there were two more sons, Jack and Luke.

Quinn cut his hockey teeth in the hothouse of Toronto for the next nine years, playing for his own Marlboros, the storied minor hockey organization that boasts Connor McDavid and John Tavares among its many alumni.

At 16, Quinn went back to play for the US National Team Development Program before signing with the University of Michigan, where he had 29 points in 37 games as a freshman. It was a big year for the kinesiology and sports management student, he also earned a bronze at the 2018 World Junior Championship and joined the men at the World Championship. The only collegiate player on the team, he added another bronze.

"I'd pay to watch him play and there aren't many players I'd say that about," said on NHL scout.

The Vancouver Canucks drafted Hughes seventh overall in 2018, and he spent another season with the Wolverines, leading the team with 28 assists and 33 points in 32 games. He signed his first professional contract late in the 2018–19 season, and the 19 year-old registered three assists in five NHL games.

A little taste of the big leagues was followed by a summer trip north to practice with Nova Scotian and NHL royalty Sidney Crosby, Nathan MacKinnon and Brad Marchand in Halifax. Hughes wasn't as star-stuck as most teens would be — Maple Leaf William Nylander had lived with the family in Toronto — but the level of skill and commitment was eye-opening.

Hughes burst on the scene in 2019–20 with 45 assists and 53 points in 68 games, unfortunately COVID-19 shortened the season. He continued his torrid pace in the postseason bubble, earning 14 assists and 16 points in 17 games, and finished second in 2020 Calder Trophy voting.

The 2020–21 season brought a realigned NHL and a bit of a sophomore slump for Hughes, who had the seventh-highest five-on-five goals against rate among defensemen and a minus-24. Some consider it an old-school stat, but it mattered to the young star.

While playing 25:15 minutes a game in 2021–22, tenth in the NHL, Hughes tied for sixth among defensemen with 68 points and fourth with 60 assists. Both eclipsed franchise records that stood for decades — Doug Lidster's 63 points in 1987 and Dennis Kearns' 55 assists in 1977. His goals-against-per-60-minutes also dropped to 2.18 at five-on-five, down from 3.27

the season prior, and he posted a plus-10.

"It sounds crazy, but I think I'm more satisfied about the plus-minus and my overall game than I am the points, honest to God," said Hughes. "The points are nice, but it was just such a hard year last year, being dash-24, and I took it personal."

The Hughes became the first American family to have three brothers taken in the first round when Luke, a defenseman, was drafted fourth overall by the New Jersey Devils in 2021, two years after they took Jack, a center, first overall.

New Jersey would love to score a Hughes hat trick, but Vancouver's not going to make a deal with the Devils. Quinn has a team-friendly six-year, $7.85 million a season contract, and he just started rewriting the Canucks' record book.

"He's a special player, but he's going to break that record five times from now," predicted head coach Bruce Boudreau. "Every year he's going to be better. For now it's cool, but he knows he's going to do a lot better in the future."

Won bronze at both the 2018 World Junior Championship and World Championship

Won silver at the 2019 World Junior Championship

Played in the 2020 NHL All-Star Game

First-team NHL All-Rookie in 2020

Three-time winner of the Canucks' Walter (Babe) Pratt Trophy as the club's best defenseman (2020–2022), the first to win the award in three straight years seasons since Ed Jovanovski from 2001 to 2003

Alex Pietrangelo wears four rubber bands around his wrist when he plays. There's a light-blue one for his niece Ellie, who beat kidney cancer; a dark-blue one for Liam, a 2-year-old heart transplant recipient he met in 2016; and then an orange one for Mandi Schwartz, sister of former teammate Jaden Schwartz, and a blue and yellow one for Seth Lange, a St. Louis teenager, both of whom died of leukemia.

The last two bands on his wrist don't represent all the people he's lost. In 2001, on Pietrangelo's 11th birthday, his friend Cosmo Oppedisano succumbed to cancer. It was an early lesson of life's cruelty.

Pietrangelo spent his early days on a backyard rink in King City, 45 minutes north of Toronto, complete with outdoor lights, bonfires and best friends. But his talent soon outgrew his town and he joined the Toronto Junior Canadiens.

Pietrangelo scored the 2005 all-Ontario bantam championship-winning goal, and through the years he and coach Tyler Cragg remained friends. Cragg continued to train Pietrangelo well into his NHL days, until he died of cancer in 2015 at the age of 44.

From the Junior Canadiens, Pietrangelo was taken third overall by the Mississauga IceDogs in the 2006 Ontario Hockey League draft. After Pietrangelo put up 105 points over two OHL seasons, the St. Louis Blues took him fourth overall in the 2008 NHL Entry Draft.

The following season he won a gold medal with Team Canada at the 2009 World Junior Championship, and a year later he had 12 points in six World Junior games and was named the tournament's best defenseman while winning silver.

In his first full NHL season, in 2010–11, the 6-foot-3, 205-pound defenseman showed he belonged permanently. He led all Blues defensemen in points (43), plus-minus (plus-18) and shots (161). Then at the 2011 World Championship, he had five points in seven games and was voted the top defenseman.

At 22, Pietrangelo became the youngest defenseman in franchise history to have consecutive seasons of 40 or more points and later became the first with at least 40 points in each of his first four full NHL seasons. Then, in 2016, the Blues officially handed him the reins.

"It makes me excited to know I could be the first captain to raise the Stanley Cup in the city of St. Louis," said Pietrangelo.

And he was, in the most unlikely fashion. The Blues were at the bottom of the standings in early January 2019 before they caught fire, riding momentum and Pietrangelo's leadership all the way to the Stanley Cup Final against the Boston Bruins.

In Game 7 Pietrangelo assisted on Ryan O'Reilly's opening goal to set a franchise record for assists in the playoffs (16), and his goal with eight seconds left in the first period stood as the 2019 Stanley Cup winner.

He finished the postseason tops among all defensemen in scoring with 19 points.

After a career high 16 goals and his second highest point total (52) in the truncated 2019–20 season, Pietrangelo couldn't come to terms with the Blues and the free agent was signed by the Vegas Golden Knights.

Following another shortened season Pietrangelo was as hot as Vegas in June in the 2021 Stanley Cup semi-final, scoring three goals and orchestrating play masterfully from the back. If not for Montreal Canadiens goalie Carey Price, he would have taken Vegas to the second Stanley Cup Final in the franchise's short history.

In 2021–22 the team failed to make the playoffs for the first time, but the ageless 14-year veteran led the team in ice time. He's now ninth among NHL defensemen in goals (128), 10th in assists (386), eighth in points (514), and seventh in average ice time (24:47) since 2010–11.

"Things aren't always going to go your way, right?" relates Pietrangelo. "So how do you go to the rink every day and enjoy yourself, and enjoy the fact that you do what you love for a living?"

Pietrangelo took that love to his third All-Star Game and won the breakaway challenge at his home rink with a Vegas-worthy performance and an assist from a friendly judge. St. Louis-born actor and hockey superfan Jon Hamm gave him 19 points (out of 10) to honor the '19 Stanley Cup.

He's always gotten by with a little help from his friends, whether they were in the stands when he won the Cup or on his wrist as he lifted it.

Won gold at the 2009 World Junior Championship

Led the 2010 WJC in goals (3), assists (9) and points (12) and named tournament's Best Defenseman

Named Best Defenseman at the 2011 World Championship

Won gold at the 2014 Olympics

Won the World Cup of Hockey in 2016

Played in three NHL All-Star Games (2018, 2020, 2022)

Won the Stanley Cup in 2019, scoring the championship-clinching goal

JACOB MARKSTROM

system, and by 18 he was the number one rated international goalie according to NHL Central Scouting.

His journey to the NHL wasn't quite as rapid. Drafted with the first pick of the second round, 31st overall, by the Florida Panthers in 2008, he didn't become an NHL regular for a decade.

Markstrom spent two more years with Brynas and in 2009–10 he led the Swedish Hockey League in the save percentage (.927) and goals against average (2.01) to win Rookie of the Year and the Honken Trophy as best goalie. He also led the 2009 World Junior Championship with a .946 save percentage and finished second in goals-against average (1.61), as Sweden took silver and he was named Top Goaltender.

After his first NHL training camp in 2010, Markstrom was sent to the American Hockey League's Rochester Americans with the expectation that he'd be in Florida soon. But North American hockey and living alone a long way from home for the first time took some getting used to, and his numbers were pedestrian.

Markstrom was with the San Antonio Rampage in 2014 when he got the call that he'd been traded to the Vancouver Canucks as part of the package for goalie and franchise icon Roberto Luongo. There was little pressure to replace a legend though, because he stayed in the AHL with the Utica Comets, where he found his groove in 2014–15. He had a 22-7-2 record, 1.88 goals-against average, .934 save percentage, and the Comets rode him to the Calder Cup final.

The following two seasons Markstrom stuck with the Canucks as Ryan Miller's backup, playing a total of 59 games while learning to be an NHL player from the Swedish contingent in Vancouver. "I had two of the best teachers in Henrik and Daniel (Sedin) when it comes to that," he said.

When Miller went to the Anaheim Ducks, Markstrom finally got his shot to be number one. He had 60 starts in each of 2017–18 and 2018–19, and he was consistently solid with goals-against averages of 2.71

Jacob Markstrom's childhood was a lesson in unstructured play. Neighborhood parents in Gavle, in eastern Sweden near the Baltic Sea, would flood the tennis courts, and the kids would skate all day. But when it thawed, hockey was out and soccer was in, especially for Markstrom.

His father was a professional soccer goalie who became the goalie coach for the Swedish national women's team, and his brother, Tim, grew up to be a pro goalie too. His sister, Ida, bucked the family tradition and played out, and his childhood idol was Swedish striker Zlatan Ibrahimovic. A tall kid who'd grow up to be 6-foot-6, being a soccer goalie would've been a natural choice for Markstrom.

Even in organized hockey, Markstrom played every position and didn't focus on goaltending until he was 14. A year later he was invited to join the Brynas

Won silver at the 2009 World Junior Championship and named Best Goaltender

Won the SHL's Honken Trophy (best goaltender) and Rookie of the Year in 2009–10

Won gold at the 2013 World Championship

Won the Cyclone Taylor Trophy as Canucks' MVP in 2019 and 2020

Played in the 2020 All-Star Game

Led the NHL with nine shutouts in 2021–22

and 2.77 and save percentages of .912 and .912.

Markstrom reached another level in 2019–20, playing in the All-Star Game and finishing fourth in Vezina Trophy voting. In the playoff bubble, he helped Vancouver beat the Minnesota Wild and defending Stanley Cup champion St. Louis Blues, but he was injured against the Vegas Golden Knights.

Hitting the free agent market after a hot year, Markstrom negotiated with Vancouver and turned down a lucrative offer from the Edmonton Oilers before signing a six-year, $36 million contract with Calgary.

They got their money's worth and then some in

2021–22. Markstrom went 37-15-9 and led the NHL with nine shutouts, surpassing the total shutouts he had from 2010 to 2020. He was third in goals-against average (2.22), tied for third in save percentage (.922), tied for fourth in wins, and a Vezina finalist.

After dispatching the Dallas Stars in seven games, with Markstrom's .943 save percentage, it was the first Battle of Alberta since 1991, and Edmonton had revenge on the mind for the goalie who spurned them. The series had scores, goalie gaffes and defense on both ends more reminiscent of the 1980s, and the Flames were eliminated in five games that felt like seven.

Markstrom had an ugly 5.12 goals-against average and an .852 save percentage in the series, and for a fiery competitor who once refused to watch game tape because he hated seeing himself scored on, it was a tough pill to swallow. But the team didn't blame him. "I would go to war with that goaltender any day of the week," said general manager Brad Treliving.

"He's the backbone of our team," agreed defenseman Chris Tanev, who also played with Markstrom in Vancouver. "He's probably our best player, and he will continue to be moving forward."

One of the most coveted assets in hockey is a big, offensively gifted yet defensively responsible center. To find such a unicorn, the Los Angeles Kings went all the way to Slovenia, a country with only 2 million people, seven rinks, and 158 men and 67 women over the age of 20 registered to play hockey.

Anze Kopitar, from Jesenice, a town in the northern part of the country near the Austrian border, is the first Slovene to play in the NHL. More common is his origin story. Playing on a backyard rink that his grandfather flooded, Anze spent hours out there pretending to be his dad, Matjaz, who was a national team player.

"He was always scoring big goals in big games, so I always wanted to be that guy, too," said Anze.

It was the biggest stage he could imagine as a boy, but when Slovenia hosted an international tournament, scouts who came to see players from the usual European hockey powers discovered a local product who could play. In 2004, at the age of 16, Kopitar left to play for Sodertalje SK in Sweden.

In 2005 Kopitar had 10 goals and 13 points for Slovenia in the B pool of the World Junior Championship, and 11 points in five games at the under-18 tournament. He also represented his country at the highest level for the first time in Olympic qualifying and at the World Championship, with his father as assistant coach.

It was the same year the Kings picked him 11th overall in the entry draft, and Kopitar made his NHL debut at 19 years old on October 6, 2006, scoring two goals against the Anaheim Ducks. In his second game he had three assists against the St. Louis Blues.

Kopitar led the Kings in scoring in 2007–08, the start of nine straight seasons that the center ranked first on the team, breaking Marcel Dionne's franchise record of eight consecutive years from 1975–76 to 1982–83.

Kopitar has 22 goals and 70 points in 86 career postseason games, including eight goals and 20 points in the 2012 playoffs, tied with then-captain Dustin Brown atop the NHL, to help lead the Kings to the franchise's first Stanley Cup.

In 2014 Wayne Gretzky, who knows something about playing in LA and being great, called Kopitar the third-best player in the world, behind Jonathan Toews and Sidney Crosby. In the playoffs Kopitar bettered them both, leading all players in assists (21) and points (26) as the Kings won their second championship.

Earlier in 2014 Slovenia defied all odds and logic by reaching the quarterfinals of the Sochi Olympics. At the helm was Kopitar, who was cut from the Yugoslavian team just before the Sarajevo Olympics in 1984 but 30 years later fulfilled his Olympic dream as head coach of Slovenia. His son was the only NHL player on the Slovenian Olympic team.

The 2015–16 season was another banner one for Kopitar, who won the Frank J. Selke Trophy as best defensive forward and the Lady Byng Trophy for being the league's most sportsmanlike player. The Kings rewarded him with an eight-year, $80 million contract in 2016. In September of that year he captained Team Europe at the World Cup of Hockey. It was the second team that named him captain that summer after the Kings gave the C to Kopitar, who had been Brown's lieutenant and alternate for eight seasons.

Fatigue from the World Cup and Olympic qualifying coupled with an arm injury led to a down year for Kopitar in 2016–17, but he bounced back in a big way with career highs in goals (35), assists (57) and points

(92) in 2017–18. It was an improvement of 40 points over the year prior, 31 points more than his closest teammate, and enough to tie him for seventh in league scoring. The career year earned Kopitar his second Selke Trophy, and he was one of three finalists for the Hart Trophy as NHL MVP.

In 2018–19 Kopitar reached 1,000 games played, and in 2021 he became the fourth King with 1,000 career points. He's led the team in scoring 14 times and by the end of 2021–22, he had accumulated 365 goals, 702 assists, and 1,067 points. He's second in franchise history in assists and fourth in goals and points, having passed Gretzky in both, and with a strong 2022–23, he could be first in assists and second in points.

Kopitar said he and Gretzky don't belong in the same sentence, but the NHL's all-time leading scorer disagrees: "We have a mutual respect for each other, and he's what you want as a face of an organization. And he not only plays the game the right way, but he's got a pretty good sense of the history of the game, growing up far away."

Played in five NHL All-Star Games (2008, 2011, 2015, 2018, 2020)

Won the Stanley Cup twice (2012, 2014)

Won the Lady Byng Trophy in 2016

Won the Frank J. Selke Trophy twice (2016, 2018)

MARK STONE

Golden Knights | Right Wing | 61

When Mark Stone was a baby, his dad, Rob, played on Saturdays at Sargent Park Arena in Winnipeg, Manitoba. Older brother Michael played on foot with some other kids beside the rink, and Mark felt left out.

"Mark wanted to play hockey, too," remembers his mother, Jackie. "But he couldn't walk. So I got him one of those walkers with wheels so he could play by moving his legs around."

It was fertile training ground for both brothers; Michael has played 12 NHL seasons as a defenseman, and Mark is a star forward.

Ultracompetitive as a youngster, Mark was studying game tapes when he was 10. When he was 14, the Brandon Wheat Kings picked him 92nd overall in the 2007 Western Hockey League bantam draft. He grew

into his lanky frame over four seasons in Brandon and had 229 points in 137 games over his final two years, including 41 goals and 123 points in 66 games in 2011–12. He also won bronze with Canada's World Junior team that year, scoring seven goals and 10 points in six games.

Drafted in the sixth round, 178th overall, in 2010 by the Ottawa Senators, two years after the Coyotes took his brother 69th overall, Stone spent two seasons shuttling between Ottawa and its AHL affiliate in Binghamton. After proactively working on his skating he established himself as an NHL regular in 2014–15 with 26 goals and 64 points.

Over the following four seasons Stone did it all — he played on special teams, shut down the opponents' stars and gave rookies a place to live. He was also consistent in his scoring and demeanor, even through Ottawa's wild ups and downs.

The Senators reached the Eastern Conference Final in 2017, but less than two years later they had plummeted all the way to the bottom of the standings. He escaped the sinking ship in Ottawa when the impending free agent was dealt to the Golden Knights at the 2019 trade deadline for a package that included Vegas' top prospect Erik Brannstrom. "Stone is the here, the now, the future," said then-Vegas general manager George McPhee.

The Golden Knights reached the Stanley Cup Final in 2018 and went all in to take that final step in 2019. Stone held up his end of the bargain; he was leading the NHL in both goals (6) and points (12) when the San Jose Sharks eliminated them in Game 7 of round one.

"There are a lot of guys that I respect in this league," said linemate Paul Stastny after Stone scored his first career hat trick in Game 3. "But the ones I respect most are the ones who think the game, and have that vision and anticipation, and think one step ahead. That's what [Stone] has."

Stone's hockey IQ covers the full extent of the ice, and he was a finalist for the 2019 Selke Trophy as the NHL's best defensive forward, a rarity for a winger. When he was on the ice for the last-place Senators in 2018–19, they were a remarkable plus-85 in shot attempts, and he finished the season with career highs in goals (33) and points (73).

Stone capped the year by leading the World Championship in goals (8) and winning tournament MVP after getting 14 points in 10 games and a silver medal.

Over the next two strange and shortened seasons, Stone remained steady, with 124 points in 120 games in 2019–20 and 2020–21. In the latter, he tied for 10th in the NHL in assists (40) and 11th in points (61). He was also named the first captain in franchise history in January 2021.

Although Stone resembles an Easter Island head, and is nearly as large at 6-foot-4 and 219 pounds, he's hardly stone-faced. He's one of the most expressive players in the NHL, which was on full display in the Stanley Cup semi-final of the COVID-realigned playoffs of 2021. Frustrated and eventually eliminated by Carey Price and the Montreal Canadiens, he couldn't hide his lament. Many a meme has been made by the many faces of Mark.

That discontent carried over. Despite playing in his first All-Star Game, the 2021–22 season was a low for Stone and Vegas; he missed a total of 45 games, most because of a back injury, and the Knights missed the playoffs for the first time.

Without their leader, that's no coincidence.

Named WHL and CHL Most Sportsmanlike Player in 2012

Named to the NHL All-Rookie Team in 2015

Won gold at the 2016 World Championship

Led the 2019 World Championship in goals (8), won silver, and named tournament MVP

Tied for third in game-winning goals (8), second in shooting percentage (21.4), and third in Selke Trophy voting in 2020–21

Played in the 2022 All-Star Game

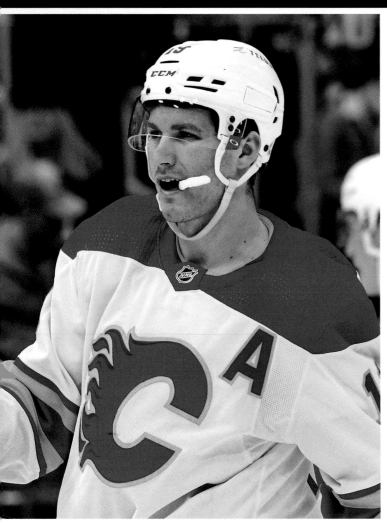

T he apples don't fall far from the Tkachuk family tree. Keith was a big, hard-nosed winger who had 1,065 points and 2,219 penalty minutes in 1,201 NHL games. His sons, Matthew and Brady, are big, hard-nosed wingers who are quickly racking up points and penalty minutes.

Born in Scottsdale, Arizona in 1997, the year after the Winnipeg Jets became the Phoenix Coyotes and few months after Keith led the NHL with 52 goals, Matthew is a dual citizen because his mother, Chantal, is from Winnipeg.

Matthew's daycare was the Coyotes' practice rink in Scottsdale. "I would drop him off, and I know the trainers would change his diapers sometimes," said Chantal.

Then-Coyotes coach Jim Schoenfeld also played

nanny, remembers Chantal: "He would let Matthew sit on the bench with a helmet on and watch practice. And he loved it so much that he would sit still the entire practice. He was probably 2 at the time."

It didn't necessarily translate to the ice. Matthew's first team was in St. Louis, after Keith was traded to the Blues. "He was so bad," according to Chantal. "He was the worst player on the team by far."

But Matthew picked up some tips from future Hall of Famer Paul Kariya in St. Louis, where Keith played for nine seasons. "It was funny because he was the skilled player and my dad was the big power forward," remembers Matthew. "Paul was always teaching me and my brother to do all this skilled stuff, and my dad was like, 'You guys are going to be power forwards.'"

It turned out to be a little of both with the U.S. National Team Development Program, winning gold at the 2015 World Under-18 Championship with a tournament high 10 assists, and in one season with the London Knights, where the fourth-round pick in the Ontario Hockey League draft turned himself into a first rounder in the NHL.

In 57 regular season games with the powerhouse Knights in 2015–16, Tkachuk had 30 goals and 107 points, and added four goals and 11 points in seven World Junior Championship games. In the playoffs he led the OHL in goals (20) and penalty minutes (42), finishing with 40 points in 18 games, and another five goals and eight points at the Memorial Cup, including the Cup-winning goal in overtime.

The Calgary Flames took Tkachuk sixth overall in 2016 and the 18-year-old was ready for primetime immediately. "I noticed it when he was a rookie — and this is not usual for young guys — he wants to be that difference-maker, that game-winner," said Mikael Backlund, Tkachuk's linemate in his first season. "And he had that confidence from a young age to know he could be."

Tkachuk has also made a few enemies around the NHL as "a pest and an agitator," former USNTDP

linemate and roommate and current Columbus Blue Jacket Jack Roslovic says fondly.

As childhood teammate and San Jose Shark Luke Kunin sees it: "He likes to get under people's skin, and a lot of the way he does that is with his skill. As far as his skill set goes, it's off the charts. The way he handles the puck, the vision, the plays he can make are almost second to none."

In 2021–22, linemates Johnny Gaudreau, Elias Lindholm and Tkachuk were first, second and third in the NHL in plus-minus, respectively, and combined for 301 points as the Flames finished first in the Pacific Division with the fourth highest points percentage in the league.

Already a six-year veteran at 24, Tkachuk shattered his previous highs in goals (42), assists (62) and points (104), finishing eighth in the NHL in points.

While Keith still has bragging rights with that 52-goal season, Matthew surpassed his dad's career high of 98 points and ended the season averaging 0.89 points a game. Keith's career average? Precisely 0.89 points a game.

After dispatching the Dallas Stars in seven games, Tkachuk had three goals in the wild 9-6 win to open

Won gold at the World Under-17 Championship (2014) and World Under-18 Championship (2015)	
Led the OHL in playoff goals (20) and scored the Memorial Cup-winning goal in 2016	
Played in the 2020 All-Star Game	
Eighth in the NHL in points (104), tied for ninth in goals (42), and third in plus-minus (+57) in 2021–22	

the Battle of Alberta, making him the first Flame with a hat trick in the playoffs since Theo Fleury in 1995, but he cooled off as the Edmonton Oilers took the series in five games.

But it was Tkachuk's last hurrah in Calgary. After Gaudreau left in free agency, Tkachuk expressed his desire to play in the U.S., and the Flames granted his wish with one of the biggest trades in recent memory, bringing back a package that included 115-point scorer Jonathan Huberdeau from the Florida Panthers. Tkachuk then signed an eight-year, $76 million extension.

"I'll always remember my time in Calgary as the most important and best years in my life," Tkachuk said afterwards. Calgarians might not remember him quite as fondly.

The list of things that Brent Burns is at or near the top of in the NHL includes thickest beard, most teeth missing, most tattoo coverage, largest menagerie and most points scored.

His annual NHL photos looks like a *Teen Wolf* transformation. And yes, his body is a colorful mosaic of art, and he once had 300 or so snakes, including some rare varieties he crossbred. But focusing on his eccentricities does a disservice to the work ethic that propelled Burns to the NHL.

"He wasn't a very elegant skater. He was bent over like a hunchback toward the ice," recalled Jari Byrski, a skills coach who first met Burns when he was 8 years old. "The thing with Brent is he was always about energy. I'm not talking about a crazy kid not paying attention. Absolutely not. When he set out to

do something, he did it the right way and didn't go half-way. He was all in."

Burns was a 5-foot-11 winger when the Brampton Battalion chose him in the third round of the 2001 Ontario Hockey League draft. When training camp started, he was 6-foot-2. "I still think of myself as a small player," said Burns, who is now 6-foot-5 and 230 pounds. "I think it helped my skating and my puckhandling."

After Burns played just one season at forward with the Battalion in 2002–03, the Minnesota Wild took him with the 20th overall selection in the 2003 NHL Entry Draft. He made quite a first impression, walking on stage in a white suit. "He looked like the guys from *Dumb and Dumber*," said Battalion coach Stan Butler.

Burns also impressed in his first NHL training

camp. He made the Wild, and his legend began to grow in Minnesota. Off the ice, he became known for his esoteric pursuits like martial arts, as well as for growing his hair and collecting reptiles; on the ice, he'd been converted into a defenseman and set a team record for blue-liners in 2010–11 with 46 points.

And as then-Wild general manager Doug Risebrough learned, "He's not totally what you see. He's carefree, not careless."

In a draft day deal in 2011, the Wild sent Burns to San Jose. The Sharks moved him back to forward during the 2012–13 season but soon realized they were better served with him on the ice more frequently.

In 2015–16 Burns set a new career high with 75 points and became just the fourth defenseman in the past 20 years to reach the 25-goal mark, scoring 27. He also joined Bobby Orr and Ray Bourque as the only defensemen with at least 350 shots in a season — his 353 were second to Alex Ovechkin's 398.

In the 2016 playoffs Burns had 24 points in 24 games as the Sharks reached their first Stanley Cup Final, ultimately losing to the Pittsburgh Penguins.

Burns spent that off-season roaming the United States on his custom-made all-black road bicycle, while his family followed in their matte black Mercedes van. He'd work out in Walmart parking lots and at the homes of people they met along the way. Finding his own Route 88 was a way to free his mind and spirit, while pushing his body outside the confines of a gym. It paid off for Burns in 2016–17. The Barrie, Ontario, native led all defensemen with 29 goals, 12 more than the next blue-liner, and 76 points, which earned him the Norris Trophy.

In 2018–19 Burns set new career highs in assists (67), good for fifth in the NHL, and points (83), both of which were first among defensemen. He led the Sharks in scoring for the second year in a row and his was the highest point total by a defenseman since Brian Leetch in 1995–96.

Following full COVID-shortened seasons of 70 games in 2019–20 and 56 in 2020–21, Burns played in all 82 games in 2021–22. He hasn't missed a game since 2013, and he finished the season 37 years-old and third in the league in average ice time at 26:09 a game.

His abilities aren't limited to durability and reliability. Burns finished 12th in scoring among defensemen with 54 points and now sits first in goals (227), assists (550), and points (777) since he entered the league, more than 100 points ahead of Erik Karlsson in second.

Burns' next adventure will be in Carolina, as a team on the rebuild dealt him to a team on the rise. The six-time All-Star leaves San Jose as the franchise leader among defensemen in goals, assists, points, power play goals, game-winning goals and shots, and brings the Hurricanes serious championship aspirations. And more than a little bit of character.

Played in six NHL All-Star Games (2011, 2015, 2016, 2017, 2018, 2019)
Won gold at the 2015 World Championship and named best defenseman
Named NHL Foundation Player of the Year in 2015
Won the 2016 World Cup of Hockey
Won the Norris Trophy in 2017

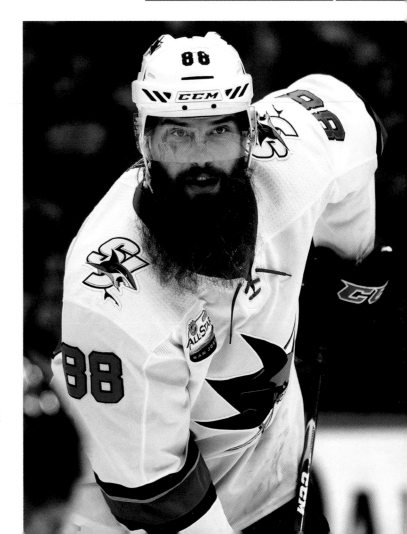

the age of 15. "I was just as good at soccer as I was at hockey," recalled Doughty. "But living in Canada, it's going to be tough to make it [in soccer] anywhere. So I kind of gave it up. I miss playing it all the time."

Paul believes the two sports worked together in his son's favor: "I actually think playing soccer helped him with hockey. He could sit back in net and watch the whole play develop in front of him."

At 17 Doughty led the Ontario Hockey League's Guelph Storm in scoring in 2006–07, with 74 points in 67 games. A year later he won the Max Kaminsky Trophy as the OHL's most outstanding defenseman and was named the top blue-liner at the 2008 World Junior Championship after Canada won gold.

Later that year LA picked Doughty second overall in the entry draft, and after his fitness was questioned he dropped 20 pounds during the summer. He made the team out of training camp and played his first game for the Kings at 18, the second-youngest defenseman in franchise history. Conditioning wasn't an issue; Doughty averaged almost 24 minutes a game his rookie year.

"[Doughty] understood the game, he understood the nuances," said Sean O'Donnell, Doughty's first NHL defense partner and mentor. "It usually takes defensemen years to do that and some never get it. To see him do that as a 19-year-old, you knew he was special."

In 2010 Doughty was a finalist for the Norris at 20 years old, the second youngest to be nominated for the award, after Bobby Orr. He had helped the Kings reach the playoffs for the first time in eight years. He was also the youngest member of Canada's gold medal Olympic team. Over the course of the tournament he moved up the depth chart to form the team's top defense tandem with Duncan Keith.

Two years later, as the Kings steamrolled their way to the franchise's first championship, Doughty's 16 points in 20 playoff games led all blue-liners, and his

Exhibit A in the argument for East Coast bias is the Kings' Drew Doughty. If hockey writers in the east couldn't stay up late enough to get a true measure of the talent in the west, they were missing out on one of the league's best players in Los Angeles.

Doughty's 2016 Norris Trophy as the NHL's best defenseman was years overdue, but the individual bauble was just icing on the cake. He'd already won every important championship (some twice) by the time it finally came his way.

Growing up in London, Ontario, Doughty dreamed of hoisting the World or FA Cups just as much as Lord Stanley's. His mother, Connie, is Portuguese and his father, Paul, is English, so soccer was a household passion.

Though Doughty was a standout soccer goalie, he made the difficult decision to focus on hockey at

26:08 of average ice time was almost a minute more than anyone else in the Stanley Cup Final.

In 2014, after adding a second gold medal to his trophy case at the Sochi Olympics, Doughty topped all defensemen again with 18 points in the playoffs as the Kings won their second Stanley Cup.

Doughty only missed three games between 2014–15 and 2020–21, and since coming into the NHL, he's third in games played and second in average ice time among defensemen, including an NHL-leading 26:23 in 2020–21 at the age of 32. But he played only 39 games in 2021–22, and his season ended early after suffering a wrist injury that required surgery. He still had 31 points, just three behind his total in the 56-game season of 2020–21, and after three seasons in the minuses, he was back to plus-four.

Doughty played his 1,000th career game in 2022, the first of his draft class to get there, and his teammates wore custom masks with his gap-toothed smile when they entered the arena.

Getting long in those remaining teeth, Doughty remains a notorious trash talker and free spirit, but he's also become a respected role model.

"He's a Hall of Famer, a great player," said Quinton Byfield, who scored his first career goal that night to make him the youngest King to score since Doughty got his first in 2008. "Just being able to share that moment with him is something I'll hold on to the rest of my life."

It's easy for Doughty to relate to the emerging star, another teenager who left southern Ontario for southern California.

"I've basically grown up in L.A., since I was 18 and moved away on my own," said Doughty. "I had to overcome a lot of things, being away from my family. I couldn't have had a better group of guys and I can't thank my teammates enough for everything they've done for me and being there for me always."

Now it's his turn to pass along the wisdom, and eventually the torch. Not that he's quite ready yet.

"He was so determined and knew he had what it took to be a successful goalie," said his mother, Danielle. "Believing when you can't always see it; that is the difference between good and great."

By 14, Demko knew he needed to move beyond the San Diego Jr. Gulls so he got on the phone and started asking prep schools for tryouts, including the famed Shattuck-St. Mary's. That didn't work, but the young man found his way to the L.A. Junior Kings and then received an offer from the Omaha Lancers of the United States Hockey League.

Danielle demurred but her son was persistent. "He waited until I finished and he said 'Mom, this doesn't happen to kids from California. You and Dad have laid a great foundation, you need to let me go.' And I sat there and I thought, 'I've gotta let him go.'"

From Nebraska Demko went to the US National Team Development Program, while finishing high school early so he could attend Boston College.

In 2013–14 Demko was the youngest player in NCAA hockey, going 16-5-3 with a 2.24 goals-against average and a .919 save percentage. The Vancouver Canucks drafted him in the second round, 36th overall, that summer. He was the second goalie taken and the highest ever by a California-born goalie, and he might have gone even sooner but rumors of impending hip surgery gave some teams pause.

Demko did go under the knife in 2015, undergoing double hip surgery to repair torn labrums and impingement. Off his feet for two months and the ice for four, he spent the time honing his mental game and he came back stronger than ever. He helped Boston College advance to the Frozen Four twice, and in his final season he had a 27-8-4 record with a 1.88 goals-against average, .935 save percentage, and 10 shutouts to break a school record set by former Canuck Cory Schneider. It was the second most in college history for a single season, and it earned him the 2016 Mike Richter Award as the NCAA's best goalie.

Growing up in the southwest corner of California, Thatcher Demko didn't even have the burgeoning hockey scene and development of Los Angeles. But with obvious talent on inline skates, his parents took him to the San Diego Ice Arena when he was four. As most kids do, he rotated positions, but he was drawn to the net.

"I think when I was little it was about the pads," says Demko. "I thought the pads were really cool."

His passion for the position grew but there weren't a lot of mentors so his first goalie coach was YouTube, which he studied religiously. The internet and self-belief got Demko to a tournament in the Czech Republic when he was 10, and at 13 he wrote out one, three, five and ten-year plans in a notebook.

Demko signed an entry-level contract with the Canucks on April 20, 2016 and played his first few professional seasons with the Utica Comets of the American Hockey League.

It was 2020 that changed everything. With Jacob Markstrom in net the Canucks won the qualifying round and the official first round of the bubble playoffs to face off against the Vegas Golden Knights. Markstrom got injured in Game 4 and Demko took over, allowing just two goals over the rest of the seven-game series, including 48 saves in Game 6 for his first NHL shutout, with a 0.64 goals-against average and a .985 save percentage.

The Canucks lost but Demko was a revelation, and it was enough for the Canucks to let Markstrom go to free agency and sign with the Calgary Flames.

After sharing the net for a season with veteran Braden Holtby, 2021–22 was Demko's first as the undisputed number one, and he played like it. Starting 60 games, he had a 33-22-7 record, a 2.72 goals-against average and a .915 save percentage.

It was the sixth-most wins in franchise history, and it earned him his first All-Star Game selection and the Cyclone Taylor Trophy as the Canucks' MVP — an impressive feat when J.T. Miller had 99 points and Quinn Hughes set single-season franchise records for assists and points by a defenseman.

Now secure in his position in the southwest corner of B.C., it's Demko filling YouTube with fundamental lessons for young goalies, and the occasional highlight reel save as he contorts his 6-foot-4 frame.

Somewhere in a hockey desert, a kid is taking notes.

- Won silver at the World Under-17 (2012) and World Under-18 (2013) Championships
- Hobey Baker finalist and winner the Mike Richter Award as the NCAA's top goaltender in 2016
- Played in the 2022 NHL All-Star Game
- Third in the NHL in saves in 2021–22 (1,799)
- Won the 2022 Cyclone Taylor Trophy as the Canucks' MVP

TIMO MEIER

Sharks | Right Wing | 28

Growing up in Herisau, Switzerland, the NHL seemed very, very far away for Timo Meier. He got his NHL education on YouTube, studying Sidney Crosby, Ilya Kovalchuk, Alexander Ovechkin and Joe Thornton, while practicing whenever he could at the local arena.

"My family lived five minutes from the ice rink, so it was easy for me to walk there after school. I think I was 4 when I got into hockey. I stepped on to the ice then and have loved it ever since," says Meier.

"If I went missing from home, my parents knew where to find me — at the rink."

When Meier was 12, he started playing against kids from the big cities like Zurich and Bern and realized

he could hold his own. The Swiss League entered the realm of possibility, if not on the ice then in operations.

At 15, Meier joined the SC Rapperswil-Jona Lakers system, whose top team plays in Switzerland's professional league. When he wasn't on the ice he was interning in the office, where his duties included answering phones and filling ticket requests.

Just a year later, Meier made the leap to a new continent and culture, joining the defending Memorial Cup champion Halifax Mooseheads of the Quebec Major Junior Hockey League for the 2013–14 season.

With the distance and time difference, Meier felt very alone, and grew up fast. After a year of adjustment and growth, he shone. In 2014–15, with 44 goals and 90 points in 61 games, adding 10 goals and 21 points in 14 playoff games and the Michael Bossy Trophy as the top prospect in the QMJHL.

The San Jose Sharks made Meier the ninth overall pick in the 2015 draft, and he spent the 2015–16 season back in the QMJHL, scoring 34 goals and 87 points in 52 games split between Halifax and the Rouyn-Noranda Huskies.

Meier's professional career started in San Jose, with the Barracuda of the American Hockey League, before he made his NHL debut just down the road from his junior stomping grounds. He scored his first NHL goal on his first NHL shot on Dec. 16, 2016 in a 4-2 win over the Canadiens in Montreal.

Thornton, who had two stints with HC Davos in Switzerland during NHL lockouts and met his wife in Switzerland, took Meier under his jumbo wing. Meier was eight months old when Thornton was picked first overall by the Boston Bruins in 1997.

"Suddenly I was skating on the same ice with a guy I'd watched play growing up," says Meier. "But he was so welcoming, so nice, and even though he's a legend, he didn't make me feel like he was someone special."

At 20, Meier landed on the Sharks' top line with Shark legend Joe Pavelski and Thornton, and the admiration was mutual. "With Timo, the ability is there — he's big, he's strong, he's fast, he can shoot. He's got the talent now and the long-term potential is very, very large," said Thornton.

In 2018, after the Sharks were eliminated in the second round of the playoffs, Meier led Switzerland to a silver medal at the World Championship, finishing with seven points in seven games. He took that confidence into 2018–19 with 30 goals and 66 points, followed by 15 points in 20 playoff games as the Sharks reached the Western Conference Final.

Meier signed a four year, $24 million contract in the offseason, but his production dipped a little over the next two seasons after Thornton and Pavelski sought greener pastures while Meier had a rotating cast of linemates.

In 2021–22, however, Meier joined the upper echelon. He had 76 points in 77 games, including five goals in a 6-2 win over the L.A. Kings, a first in franchise history. He had a hat trick in the first period and two more in the second, more than justifying his selection as the Sharks' lone representative in the All-Star Game a few weeks later.

Meier led the Sharks in points, but the team missed the playoffs for the third straight season. With his contract expiring in 2023, management has to decide whether to sign their young leader to a long-term deal or cash in as he's hitting his prime.

Wherever he lands he'll sell tickets, and not from behind a desk.

Won the 2015–16 Michael Bossy Trophy as the QMJHL's top draft prospect

Memorial Cup All-Star Team in 2016

Won a silver medal with Switzerland at the 2018 World Championships

Played in the 2022 NHL All-Star Game

Became the first player in Sharks history to score five goals in a game on Jan. 17, 2022, and just the fifth in the NHL since 2000

East Palestine, Ohio, is a football town. About an hour northwest of Pittsburgh, the Miller family was a fan of all teams in black and gold but particularly the Steelers. It wasn't until the high-flying Penguins won Stanley Cups in 1991 and 1992 that father Dennis really got into hockey, which he passed onto his son, Jonathan Tanner.

J.T. Miller got his first pair of skates before he turned two and learned to use them on the backyard rink his dad built. By kindergarten he was playing with kids two and three years older, and the hockey prodigy made the local news when he was six.

Big, strong and fast, with soft hands and keen vision, Miller was as complete a player as the US National Team Development Program had seen when he joined in 2009. He was also hot-tempered and occasionally petulant. His coaches knew he was a good kid at heart, but it would take him a while to figure it out.

Drafted 15th overall by the New York Rangers in 2011, in 2012 Miller scored his first two NHL goals in his second game and his first at Madison Square Garden, endearing himself to the home fans by doing it against the New York Islanders.

That success was fleeting, however, and Miller spent more time in the American Hockey League than the NHL. "Young and dumb," by his own admission, he thought he knew better than Rangers coach John Tortorella, a man not known for tolerating dissent.

Loaned to Team USA for the 2013 World Junior Championship, Miller tied for the team lead with nine points in seven games and won gold.

At his next training camp Miller had a second chance to make a first impression with new Rangers coach Alain Vigneault, but he arrived out of shape. It was a harbinger of things to come; he was demoted for the sixth time late in the 2013–14 season after missing curfew in Vancouver and had to watch as the Rangers lost the Stanley Cup Final to the Los Angeles Kings.

Called out in the media by Vigneault, Miller was embarrassed and angry. He now sees it as a necessary wake up call, but it was another authority figure who really had an impact at the time.

"I was like, 'If you keep doing the same thing, you're going to get the same result so look in the mirror, think about what you're doing,'" recalls his mother, Jen.

Motivated by mom, Miller arrived in New York six weeks early for his next training camp and learned to practice just as hard as he played. He played all 82 games in 2015–16 and 2016–17, hitting 56 points in the latter.

Miller scored the overtime winner for the Rangers in the 2018 Winter Classic before he was traded at the deadline to the Tampa Bay Lightning, where his next lesson began.

Miller signed a five-year deal with the Lightning and thought he deserved more responsibility, but playing with the team that would blossom into two-time Stanley Cup champions he had to accept a lesser role. The perfectionist was harder on himself during his Tampa tenure than anyone else and became his own worst enemy.

In the offseason Miller was traded to the Vancouver Canucks. He showed up in the best shape of his life and started to tap into all his potential with 72 points in 69 games in 2019–20.

Still passionate and strong-willed, Miller publicly questioned the NHL and the Players' Association over return to play conditions in 2021. After the Canucks dealt with 25 cases of Covid-19 and were sidelined for three weeks, the schedule had them playing two games in less than 24 hours and 19 games in 31 days. He took a stand and their schedule was altered.

In 2021–22, a decade after being drafted, Miller finally brought all the parts of his game together. He had 99 points, ninth in the NHL, 31 ahead of his closest teammate, and the most by any Canuck since Daniel Sedin won the Art Ross Trophy in 2011. He hit the 30-goal mark for the first time and smashed his career high with 67 assists, sixth in the NHL, while taking over as Vancouver's number one center after spending much of his NHL career on the wing.

He also had an A stitched on his sweater. "I take a lot of pride in wearing it," said Miller. "I never really thought I could get to this point."

Won gold at the Under-17 (2010) and Under-18 World Championship (2011)

Won gold at the 2013 World Junior Championship

Won the Canucks' Pavel Bure Award for most exciting player, the Three Stars Award, and the Cyrus H. McLean Trophy as the team's leading scorer in 2022

L ove him or hate him, Trevor Zegras was a much-needed breath of fresh air in his rookie season.

Zegras grew up in Bedford, New York, obsessed with hockey and the New York Rangers, although his favourite player was the Chicago Blackhawks' Patrick Kane. As a 10-year-old, he met Kane after a Blackhawks game, and a few years later followed in his footsteps to the USA Hockey's National Team Development Program.

"I love everything about Kaner's game," says Zegras. "He can slow it down or pick up the speed. He was really good on the power play and had all the spin-o-rama passes and played with a little bit of flair and a little bit of flash."

After being picked ninth overall by the Anaheim Ducks in 2019, Zegras spent a year with Boston University, where he had 36 points in 33 games and was named to Hockey East's All-Rookie team.

"He's a playmaker," assessed Terriers coach Albie O'Connell. "He's been touched with the gift of vision and timing and ability to find a small little window to get that puck through."

At the 2020 World Junior Championships Zegras used that talent to lead the U.S. in scoring with nine points in five games, all assists, while playing out of position on the wing. He also led the tournament in assists, each one primary.

A year later and playing at center, Zegras had seven goals and 18 points in seven World Junior games, tied for the most points by any player in the 21st century. He also equalled Jordan Schroeder's American record for career points with 27, which he managed in seven fewer games. The U.S. took gold and Zegras was a no-brainer as tournament MVP.

Ducks fans were drooling, but Zegras was sent to the American Hockey League after the tournament. His 21 points in 17 games with the San Diego Gulls had him tied for the league lead in scoring when he was called up in February 2021, a month before he turned 20.

Zegras made a name for himself early in his first full NHL season with one of the more unique assists in recent memory. In a win over the Buffalo Sabres, he scooped up the puck behind the net and lobbed it over for teammate Sonny Milano to bunt in.

Some called it a "Michigan assist," based on the "The Michigan," named for a goal made famous by Wolverine Mike Legg in 1996. Also known as a lacrosse-style goal, the player scoops the puck up behind the net and cradles it on the blade before reaching around and stuffing it into the top of the net.

Which is exactly what Zegras did a month later against the Montreal Canadiens.

Plays like that earned Zegras a special invitation to the breakaway challenge at the All-Star weekend skills competition. Dressed in the Average Joes uniform from the movie *Dodgeball*, he dodged balls as he did a spin-o-rama of his own, with the puck defying gravity and sticking to his blade before he fired it into the corner. It would've been theatrical and impressive if he wasn't blindfolded. That just made it unfathomable.

In a league that hasn't always celebrated personality and creativity, Zegras plays with unapologetic joie de vivre.

Not everyone appreciates it, however. In a game against the Arizona Coyotes, Zegras shot a puck between his legs, got his own rebound behind the net, scooped it up and scored his second Michigan of the season, wrapping his stick around Milano in the

process for an added degree of difficulty.

Jay Beagle, self-appointed guardian of hockey's outdated code, crosschecked Zegras hard from behind after he drove the net late in that meaningless game. Beagle then broke an unwritten rule of his own, beating down Troy Terry, who came to his teammate's defense and whose hands are built for goals, not fisticuffs.

Terry is three years older and had six more points than Zegras' 61 in 2021–22. The two were the top scorers on the team and will determine how high this generation of Ducks can fly.

For Calder Trophy finalist Zegras, the sky's the limit.

Named to the NCAA Hockey East All-Rookie Team and a third team All-Star in 2019–20

Won gold with the USA at the 2021 World Junior Championships, where he led the tournament in scoring and was named tournament MVP

Named to the 2021–22 All-Rookie Team

"He worked harder than anybody else to prove others wrong, to prove that he belonged," said Red Wings assistant coach Cyril Bollers.

He didn't just belong, he shone. Nurse went on to play for the Don Mills Flyers, a program with too many NHL alumni to name, and he was taken third overall by the Sault Ste. Marie Greyhounds in the 2011 Ontario Hockey League draft. In 2012–13 he had 12 goals and 29 assists and added 116 penalty minutes in 68 games with the Greyhounds before being drafted seventh overall by the Edmonton Oilers in 2013.

Nurse spent two more years in the Soo, and in 2015 he won gold at the World Junior Championship with future Edmonton teammate and Hart Trophy winner Connor McDavid, who he then faced a few months later in the OHL's Western Conference Final, with McDavid's Erie Otters winning in six games.

Sent to the American Hockey League out of training camp in 2015, Nurse only spent nine games in the minors. He played 69 NHL games in 2015–16, and by 2018–19 he was living up to his potential with career highs in assists (31) and points (41).

The Oilers failed to qualify for the postseason in three of Nurse's first four seasons, with the weight of missing the playoffs 12 out of 13 years hanging over the franchise, but with McDavid and Nurse leading a young core, hope sprang eternal.

Hope, however, can be a dangerous thing. Back in the pandemic-impacted playoffs in 2020 and playing at home in the Edmonton bubble, the Oilers lost to the Chicago Blackhawks, the lowest seed in their bracket, in the qualifying round.

That disappointment motivated Nurse to return to the Burlington Pond, his first arena, to work with Michele Moore Davison, a former world champion synchronized skater and the daughter of the skating coach who'd taught Nurse since he was seven. Already fleet of foot, Nurse got more explosive and efficient.

D arnell Nurse isn't the best player on his hockey team. He's probably not even the best athlete in his family.

Darnell's father, Richard, played for their hometown Hamilton Tiger-Cats in the Canadian Football League and his mother, Cathy, played basketball at McMaster University. One sister, Kia, won two NCAA basketball titles and plays for the Phoenix Mercury of the WNBA and Team Canada, and his other, Tamika, also played NCAA basketball. His cousin, Sarah, is a double Olympic medalist in hockey, including gold at the 2022 Games, and his uncle by marriage is Donovan McNabb, formerly a Pro Bowl NFL quarterback.

With sports in the blood, Darnell started skating at age four and found his way to the Toronto Red Wings, an out-of-towner and rare Black kid on the ice.

Nurse also enlisted friend Jorge Blanco, a kickbox-ing champion and Olympic boxer, to up his endurance level.

The extra work paid off in 2020–21. Nurse was second in goals scored among defensemen (16) and first in even-strength goals (15). He was also seventh in the NHL with a plus-27, fourth in average ice time (25:38), and first in defensive point shares (5.2).

But that was followed by a sweep at the hands of the Winnipeg Jets in the first round of the 2021 playoffs, including three overtime games. Nurse played 62:07 in Game 4, the third-highest ever recorded in a single game, and later that night, he and partner Mikayla welcomed their first child into the world.

On the eve of the 2021–22 season, Nurse signed a contract that will pay him $9.25 million annually for eight years, and when you're paid like a superstar, expectations rise and the lights get brighter.

The unquestioned number one defenseman on the Oilers played the hard minutes to prove it, and a long season was followed by playoff success. The Oilers beat the Los Angeles Kings in round one and took out the Calgary Flames in the second round, before a sweep at the hands of the Colorado Avalanche.

Won the Bobby Smith Trophy for OHL Scholastic Player of the Year in 2012–13

Won gold at the 2012 Ivan Hlinka Memorial tournament

Won gold at the 2015 World Junior Championship

Won silver at the 2019 World Championship

Blamed for some of the ugly playoff numbers — a 9-6 loss to Calgary and an 8-6 defeat to Colorado in consecutive series-opening games — it was revealed after the Oilers were eliminated that Nurse was playing against the NHL's best with a torn hip flexor.

But it wasn't just heavy usage that weighed on Nurse. Asked about racism in hockey, he was appre-hensive but took the challenge head on.

The former OHL Scholastic Player of the Year is more comfortable letting his actions do the talking, and in his continued effort to help others shine he created the Darnell Nurse Excellence Scholarship at St. Thomas More, his Hamilton alma mater. "You just want these young adults to get the most out of their high school experience, to take what they learned from those times, and go out and make a difference in the world," he explained.

It's something Darnell and the Nurses are very familiar with.

S hea Theodore learned to skate at the Aldergrove Community Arena, the only rink in the British Columbia town of about 15,000 people. And it's where he played all his hockey through midget, even when bigger teams came calling.

"A lot of kids moved and went to play for winter clubs or that, but I just stayed because I liked my friends and I liked playing close to home," said Theodore. "We only had 24 kids try out for the team every year. Everyone pretty much made the team."

Theodore finally left his hometown after being drafted by the Western Hockey League's Seattle Thunderbirds in 2010. At the tender age of 15, he led the Thunderbirds defense with 35 points, then upped that total to 50 and 79 points in the next two seasons.

Drafted 26th overall by the Anaheim Ducks in 2013 Theodore seemed poised to play in 2014, but he was injured in training camp and sent back to junior. It was a personal blow but a blessing to his country.

Eligible for the 2015 World Juniors, Theodore was on the top defensive pair with Darnell Nurse. The tandem didn't allow a goal the entire tournament and Canada won gold for the first time in six years.

Theodore spent the following two seasons bouncing between the NHL and AHL, playing 53 games over two seasons with the Ducks before being traded to the Vegas Golden Knights during the 2017 expansion draft.

The motley crew of castoffs in Sin City made an unprecedented and entertaining run all the way to the Stanley Cup Final, with Theodore earning 10 points in the playoffs, including the first postseason goal in franchise history, against the Los Angeles Kings.

The Golden Knights were vanquished in five games by the Washington Capitals, but the team won over a city, and Theodore had an NHL home, signing a seven-year, $36.4 million contract in the off-season.

A midseason move to the right side in 2018–19, where Theodore played in his last two seasons in Seattle, helped the left-shooting defender become even deadlier. He had 12 points and was plus-4 in his first 21 games on the right and finished the season leading the Golden Knights' defense with 12 goals and 37 points. His already strong possession numbers also went up after the switch. He had a 57.1 percent Corsi, identical to Norris Trophy winner Mark Giordano.

Impressive, but nothing compared to his fight later that year. Theodore was diagnosed with testicular cancer at just 24 after anomalies in blood and drug tests he took while winning silver at the 2019 World Championship.

Surgery removed a tumour, but he was reticent

about opening up to loved ones and the team, until the support started pouring in. He realized he was uniquely positioned to be an advocate for young men facing the same disease.

"Whether or not you believe everything happens for a reason, what happened to me really feels like a miracle," said Theodore.

With a new lease on life and motivated by a donation he made for each point to early detection causes, Theodore upped his point total to 46 in eight fewer

games played in 2019–20. He was also part of the defense that allowed the fewest goals in the NHL.

Theodore nearly equalled that with 42 points in only 53 games of the shortened 2020–21 season, while tying for fifth in the NHL in plus-minus (plus-28).

In 2021–22 Theodore had career-highs with 52 points and 14 goals, tied for seventh in the NHL among defensemen. Five of those were game-winners, including a stretch of three over eight games as Vegas fought to get into the playoffs.

The son of Aldergrove is healthy and hitting his prime at 27, while making an impact in his community and beyond. He started "Kay's Power Play" to fund early breast cancer detection and honor his grandmother, who dropped the ceremonial faceoff puck at a Golden Knights "Hockey Fights Cancer" game in 2019 and lost her own battle in 2020.

Theodore knows there's more to life than wins and losses: "It's all about supporting one another and cherishing each day and every moment with each other."

Won gold at the 2012 Hlinka Gretzky Cup, 2013 Under-18 World Championship and 2015 World Junior Championship

Named WHL West first-team All-Star and Bill Hunter Trophy winner as the league's best defenseman in 2015

Scored the first goal in Golden Knights' playoff history (April 11, 2018, against the Los Angeles Kings)

Won silver at the 2019 World Championship

First in the NHL in expected plus-minus (+27.7) in 2019–20 and tied for fifth in plus-minus (+28) in 2020–21

B orn in the Bavarian town of Rosenheim, southeast of Munich near the Austrian border, Philipp Grubauer took up hockey while most of his friends and fellow Germans were playing soccer. He started on defense and switched between there and the crease until he was 14.

"Not to toot my own horn, but I could skate well and shoot a little bit," according to Grubauer.

Stopping shots proved to be his true talent. At 16, Grubauer was drafted 25th by the Belleville Bulls in the Ontario Hockey League's 2008 import draft.

In 2009, at the age of 17, he represented his country at the World Junior Championships. Germany was relegated, but at the 2010 second tier tournament, he led

them back up after posting a sparkling .974 save percentage, 0.64 goals against average, and a 5-0-0 record.

During the 2009–10 season, the Bulls traded Grubauer to the loaded Windsor Spitfires. Full of future NHLers, he was a corner piece of a championship puzzle with a 16-1-1 playoff record as Windsor won the OHL title and the Memorial Cup.

It was the summer of Grubauer as the Washington Capitals chose him in the fourth round of the 2010 NHL draft (112th overall). After one more season in the OHL with the Kingston Frontenacs, he joined the Capitals' system, spending a year in the East Coast Hockey League and another bouncing between the ECHL and the American Hockey League.

Grubauer made his NHL debut with the big club on Feb. 27, 2013, but it took him a while to establish himself after being sent back down to hone his craft. "I didn't see it as a step back, I saw it as an opportunity to take my time and develop," he said. "The NHL was always the goal, but you have to be patient."

In 2017–18, Grubauer started 28 games as Braden Holtby's backup, with a 15-10-3 record and a team-leading three shutouts. He flashed his true potential from Nov. 24 until the end of the season, when he was first among goalies with a minimum of 20 games played in goals against average (1.93) and save percentage (.937).

Grubauer started two games in the 2018 postseason to help the Capitals win the first Stanley Cup championship in franchise history. He brought the Cup back to Rosenheim, sporting lederhosen for the celebration in the town square and at the arena of his former team, Starbulls Rosenheim.

Hard against the cap, the Capitals traded Grubauer and Brooks Orpik to the Colorado Avalanche in the offseason. His best year came in the COVID-truncated 2020–21 season, going 30-9-1 with a league-leading 1.95 goals-against average and a .922 save percentage to backstop Colorado to the Presidents' Trophy.

The Avalanche were upset in the second round despite Grubauer's 1.87 goals against average in the playoffs.

After finishing third in Vezina Trophy voting, Grubauer was unable to come to terms with the Avalanche, who were cash-strapped after signing captain Gabriel Landeskog and star defenseman Cale Makar.

"He was an unbelievable goalie for us, an unbelievable teammate, one of the hardest-working guys in the room on a daily basis and I wish him nothing but the best," said Landeskog.

The grateful Seattle Kraken signed Grubauer to a six-year, $35.4 million contract a week after their expansion draft, landing the biggest fish in the free agent goalie market to anchor the new team.

"It's such a cool experience building an organization from the ground up and being there from Day 1," reasoned Hall of Fame player and Kraken general manager Ron Francis.

"You can be part of something great here, to be part of history," agreed Grubauer.

Playing at the sparkling new Climate Pledge Arena — the world's first net zero arena, where even the ice surface is rainwater — it was too much to ask Grubauer to put up a lot of zeroes in net with the expansion team, but he did make team history with the franchise's first shutout.

From Bavaria to Washington D.C., over the Rockies to Washington state and the Emerald City, Grubauer went west to find his fortune. Given the longest contract on the new team, the fortunes of the Kraken and the hopes for the city's first Stanley Cup since the Seattle Metropolitans in 1917 now ride on the slender shoulders of the 6-foot-1 German.

Memorial Cup champion (Windsor Spitfires, 2010)

Stanley Cup champion (Washington Capitals, 2018)

Tied for first in the NHL in shutouts (7), second in wins (30) and goals against average (1.95), and third in Vezina Trophy voting in 2020–21

Earned the first shutout in Kraken franchise history in a 3-0 win over the New York Islanders on Feb. 2, 2022

One of only three German goalies to win at least 100 NHL games (after Olaf Kolzig and Thomas Greiss)

PLAYER INDEX

PHOTO CREDITS

Associated Press
Bebeto Matthews: 69
John Bazemore: 159
Karl B DeBlaker: 68
Phelan Ebenhack: 158

Icon Sportswire
Andrew Bershaw: 5, 92, 119
Bailey Hillesheim: 87, 107, 113, 144
Brett Holmes: 41, 73, 98, 118, 124, 132, 136
Chris Williams : 152
Curtis Comeau: 14, 123, 127, 153
Danny Murphy: 90, 94, 108, 146
David Kirouac: 18, 28, 30, 54, 86

Derek Cain: 21, 23, 26, 37, 59, 63, 67, 89, 100, 103, 110, 125, 128, 130, 133, 145, 155
Devin Manky: 148
Douglas Stringer: 137
Dustin Bradford: 93
Fred Kfoury III: 22, 34, 51, 56, 66, 74, 81
Gavin Napier: 149
Gerry Angus: 24, 91, 112
Greg Thompson: 8, 79
Jaylynn Nash: 32
Jeanine Leech: 10, 25, 45, 46, 47, 55, 58, 60, 61, 80, 122, 131
Jeff Chevrier: 101
Jeff Halstead: 157
Jerome Davis: 40

Joel Auerbach: 27, 43
John Cordes: 151
John McCreary: 70
Joshua Bessex: 78
Joshua Lavallee: 135
Joshua Sarner: 50, 57, 62
Julian Avram: 29
Keith Gillett: 115, 126, 141, 150
Kevin Abele: 105, 116
Mark LoMoglio: 11
Matt Cohen: 35, 140, 147, 154
Matthew Pearce: 102
Melissa Tamez: 76, 104
Mingo Nesmith: 16
Nick Turchiaro: 13
Nick Wosika: 53
Nicole Fridling: 71
Patrick Gorski: 96, 97

Peter Joneleit: 9, 42
Randy Litzinger: 17, 41, 64
Richard A. Wittaker: 39, 65, 84, 134, 143
Rich Graessle: 19, 31, 71, 77
Rick Ulreich: 106, 129, 138
Rob Curtis: 109, 117, 142
Roy K. Miller: 15, 20, 36
Russell Lansford: 88, 98
Scott W. Grau: 33
Steven King: 38, 139, 156
Steven Kingsman: 95
Terrence Lee: 85
Tim Spyers: 111
Tony Quinn: 49
Vincent Ethier: 12, 48
Zachary BonDurant: 115

ACKNOWLEDGMENTS

Thank you...

De'Aira Anderson and the Seattle Kraken for the hospitality.

Darcy Shea, who almost single-handedly willed this book into existence and kept it from being another pandemic-induced publishing casualty.

And Christine, forever and always (I'm always here).

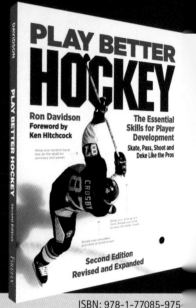

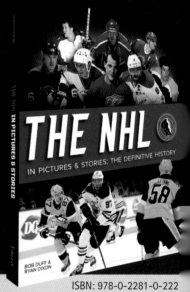